Paying
Less Tax

Paying
Less Tax

*How to keep more of your
money for saving or investing*

JOHN WHITELEY
2000 edition

How To Books

Acknowledgements
Crown Copyright material is reproduced with the permission of the controller of HMSO.

Disclaimer
Neither the author nor the publishers can be held responsible for any action taken or refrained from being taken as a result of the contents of this book.

Published by How To Books Ltd.,
3 Newtec Place, Magdalen Road,
Oxford OX4 1RE, United Kingdom
Tel: 01865 793806   Fax: 01865 248780
email: info@howtobooks.co.uk
www.howtobooks.co.uk

British Library Cataloguing-in-Publication Data
A catalogue record for this book is available from the British Library

Edited by Alison Wilson
Cover design by Shireen Nathoo Design
Cover image PhotoDisc
Cover copy by Sallyann Sheridan

Produced for How To Books by Deer Park Productions
Typeset by Concept Communications (Design & Print) Ltd, Crayford, Kent.
Printed and bound by Cromwell Press, Trowbridge, Wiltshire.

NOTE: The material contained in this book is set out in good faith for general guidance and no liability can be accepted for loss or expense incurred as a result of relying in particular circumstances on statements made in the book. The laws and regulations are complex and liable to change, and readers should check the current position with the relevant authorities before making personal arrangements.

Contents

List of Illustrations

Preface

Mr Silas P Fatcat (name changed to protect the innocent) earns over £1 million a year, has a personal fortune of over £100 million, and never pays any tax, and it is all quite legal. He is one of that élite band of people – the modern urban myth. We usually hear about him from a friend at the pub, who knows from a friend of a friend that his facts are really really true. In my experience, he is entirely fictional.

Someone once said that there are two things in life which are inescapable – death and taxes. I cannot claim to do anything about the first, but there may be some scope to reduce the impact of the second.

I do hope that this book will make you think more about the tax consequences of the way you organise your financial affairs and your business. This book does not advocate any kind of tax evasion, but it highlights ways to plan your affairs that are perfectly legal, and will lead to greater tax efficiency.

A great many professionals make a good living out of tax planning for clients. Indeed, any self-employed person who engages an accountant is, knowingly or unknowingly, engaging someone to do his tax planning for him.

The ideas in this book range from the extremely simple to steps which may need some advance planning and co-operation from other people. I have included throughout this book HOW? boxes. These explain, after each idea or method of tax saving, how to go about doing it. They are the 'nuts and bolts' of the book. There are also numerous questions and answers, and case studies root the book in real-life situations.

This book will not make you a millionaire overnight. But if you want to keep more of your hard-earned money for yourself, you may find it useful.

John Whiteley

1

Deciding Your Approach

Of all debts men are least willing to pay taxes.
Everywhere they think they get their money's worth, except for taxes.

Ralph Waldo Emerson

You are about to embark on a book about saving tax. Beware! This could prove to involve more of your life than just your financial arrangements. As with most things, a decision about one part of your life spills over to other parts. You could end up by re-evaluating your lifestyle.

You may have to pause over certain parts of the book and ask, 'Is this what I really want to do?' You may decide to throw yourself wholeheartedly into all the tax-saving ideas. You may want to pick and choose the ones which relate to your circumstances. You may wish to bend your circumstances to take advantage of some of the tax-saving opportunities.

MAKING YOUR LIFE PLANS

You may take the attitude that tax is only a secondary matter. What matters most is what you want to do with your life. This is certainly a very wise attitude. If you ran your whole life on the basis of tax efficiency, it would truly be a case of the tail wagging the dog.

However, if you have embarked on a career, with a definite aim for your life, there may be occasions when you could do things in a more tax-efficient manner, without getting the whole thing out of proportion. It makes no sense at all to neglect taking a few simple steps which could reduce your tax burden. In a judgement of a tax case which went to trial, a judge made the famous remark that nobody is under any obligation to order their affairs so that the Inland Revenue can put their biggest shovel into that person's wealth.

DECIDING ON SCHEMES

From time to time you may see or hear of special schemes promoted as tax mitigation schemes. There are two types.

Officially sponsored schemes such as **TESSAs, PEPs** or **ISAs** are government-backed. They are schemes which have been devised by the government to encourage certain types of savings, or savings in general. By all means take advantage of these if you have enough money.

The second type are **privately sponsored schemes**. They are promoted by organisations which think they have found a loophole which they can exploit. You may see them advertised in the 'quality' press, or by private circulation of clients of tax lawyers, accountants or investment houses. Be a little more wary of these. There may well be a cost for joining the scheme. The scheme may have been tried and tested, or it may be untried. Get advice – and make sure it is independent advice. Very often these schemes are targeted by the Inland Revenue, and outlawed in the next Budget. Normally, such legislation is not retrospective, so if you have 'got in on' a scheme before it is outlawed, your tax advantages are safe.

TAKING ADVICE FROM PROFESSIONALS

If you are in business, you will probably have an accountant. Do not look on him or her as just a glorified book-keeper. A qualified accountant can probably save you money in many ways – and saving tax is just one of them.

Qualified or not?
Anybody can set up in business as an accountant. But only people who are members of the relevant institutes or associations may call themselves **Chartered Accountants** or **Certified Accountants**. Unqualified accountants may be cheaper. However, qualified accountants have gone through a rigorous process of training to become qualified, and they must continue to undergo a programme of professional education. They are also bound by strict ethical codes, and are subject to disciplinary procedures if they fall short, or if a complaint against them is upheld. In addition they are required to take out professional indemnity insurance to cover claims against them.

Specific advice
If you are a 'high net worth' individual, you may also find it useful to take advice on an *ad hoc* basis for particular problems. For example, you

may be contemplating selling an asset, and want to know the capital gains tax implications. You may want to know how to pass on your wealth to the next generation of your family, and whether you can do it now, or if it has to wait until you die.

An accountant or tax lawyer could be of great use in such circumstances. Very often, the saving to you can far outweigh his or her fee.

Sometimes, a specific action, such as making a **trust**, which could be used as part of your tax-saving plans, will need a solicitor to implement it, by drawing up a trust deed, for example. It may be also that a **life assurance policy** could be taken out as part of planning for inheritance tax. It would be useful to consult an independent financial advisor about life assurances.

AND FINALLY...

Do not let the tail wag the dog. The purpose of paying less tax is to have more left in your own pocket.

There is no benefit to you in incurring an expenditure purely for the purpose of getting tax relief. The maximum tax rate is 40 per cent for income tax and capital gains tax. It is of no use to spend £100 simply to save £40 tax. You are still worse off to the tune of £60.

There is sometimes a reason for bringing forward expenditure or putting it back, so that it is relieved in the tax year which is most beneficial to you (so long as it is expenditure you would have made anyway). But never be tempted to spend money you would not otherwise have spent just so that you can get the tax relief.

CASE STUDIES
Alan relies on his accountant

Alan is self-employed, running a small business. He decides that he will concentrate on building up his business. He will leave all the tax planning to his accountant. He considers that he pays enough to his accountant, and he should therefore get a good service in terms of claiming all that is valid and in the planning of his affairs to minimise his tax bill.

Clive actively manages his tax affairs

Clive is retired, and has income from a pension and some investments. He is married. His wife does not have a large income of her own. He wants to take an active interest in his tax affairs, and will try to do all he can to save tax, and to pass on his estate to his family when he dies.

Mary takes an intelligent interest

Mary is in her 20s, and has recently married. She is employed, and quite ambitious. She and her husband do not intend to start a family yet. She does not see great scope for taking active steps to save tax. However, her work is in the financial field, and she takes an interest in anything to do with money. She intends to put a lot into her retirement fund, and further on in her career will be very interested to follow any guidance to save tax.

2

Paying Less Income Tax – 1

*The art of taxation consists in so plucking the goose as to obtain
the largest possible amount of feathers with the
smallest possible amount of hissing.*
Jean Baptiste Colbert (Minister of finance under Louis XIV)

Tax allowances are claimed by completing the right part of your self-assessment tax return. The first and most obvious way to pay less tax is to make sure that you claim all the allowances to which you are entitled. The allowances available are:

- personal allowance

- higher age-related personal allowance

- transitional allowance

- married couple's allowance (until April 2000)

- higher age-related married couple's allowance (until April 2000)

- widow's bereavement allowance (until April 2000)

- additional personal allowance

- blind person's allowance.

HOW?
Allowances are claimed by completing the appropriate box on page 6 of your self assessment tax return. See Figure 1.

USING YOUR ALLOWANCES

Personal allowance
This allowance is given to everybody. You do not have to reach any particular age to qualify: it is given to you from the moment you are born. For the 2000/2001 tax year, the personal allowance is £4,385. As we shall see further on, it is a key element in planning to pay less tax.

ALLOWANCES *for the year ended 5 April 2000*

Q16 You get your personal allowance of £4,335 automatically. **If you were born before 6 April 1935, enter your date of birth in box 21.4** - you may get higher age-related allowances.

Do you want to claim any of the following allowances?   NO   YES

If yes, please read pages 23 to 26 of your Tax Return Guide and then fill in boxes 16.1 to 16.28 as appropriate.

Date of registration (if first year of claim)   Local authority (or other register)

■ *Blind person's allowance*   16.1 / /   16.2

■ *Transitional allowance (for some wives with husbands on low income if received in earlier years).*

- Tick to claim and give details in the 'Additional information' box on page 8
  (please see page 23 of your Tax Return Guide for what is needed)   16.3

- If you want to calculate your tax, enter the amount of transitional allowance you can have in box 16.4   16.4 £

■ *Married couple's allowance for a married man* - see page 24 of your Tax Return Guide.

- Wife's full name   16.5
  - Date of marriage (if after 5 April 1999)   16.6 / /
  - Wife's date of birth (if before 6 April 1935)   16.7 / /
  - Tick box 16.8 if you or your wife have allocated **half** the allowance to her   16.8

  box number 16.9 is not used
  - Tick box 16.10 if you and your wife have allocated **all** the allowance to her   16.10

■ *Married couple's allowance for a married woman* - see page 24 of your Tax Return Guide.

  - Date of marriage (if after 5 April 1999)   16.11 / /
- Husband's full name   16.12
  - Tick box 16.13 if you or your husband have allocated **half** the allowance to you   16.13

  box number 16.14 is not used
  - Tick box 16.15 if you and your husband have allocated **all** the allowance to you   16.15

■ *Additional personal allowance (available in some circumstances if you have a child living with you - see page 25 of your Tax Return Guide).*

- Tick box 16.16A if you are claiming the married couple's allowance **and** additional personal allowance because your spouse was unable to look after themselves because of illness or disablement, throughout the year ended 5 April 2000   16.16A

- Name of the child claimed for   16.16
  - Child's date of birth   16.17 / /
  - Tick if child lived with you for at least part of the year ended 5 April 2000   16.18

- Name of university etc/type of training if the child is 16 or over on 6 April 1999 and in full time education or training   16.19

Sharing a claim

Name and address of other person claiming

16.20

Postcode

- Enter your share as a percentage   16.21 %
- If share not agreed, enter the number of days in the year ended 5 April 2000 that the child lived with
  - you   16.22 days
  - other person   16.23 days

■ *Widow's bereavement allowance*   • Date of your husband's death   16.24 / /

■ *Transfer of surplus allowances* - see page 26 of your Tax Return Guide before you fill in boxes 16.25 to 16.28.

- Tick if you want your spouse to have your unused allowances   16.25
- Tick if you want to have your spouse's unused allowances   16.26

Please give details in the 'Additional information' box on page 8 - see page 26 of your Tax Return Guide for what is needed.

If you want to calculate your tax, enter the amount of the surplus allowance you can have.

- Blind person's surplus allowance   16.27 £
- Married couple's surplus allowance   16.28 £

SPECIMEN

Fig. 1. Page 6 of self assessment tax return.

Tax tip
Make sure that, as far as possible, you and everybody in your family use up your personal tax allowance.

The personal allowance is usually increased each year by at least the same percentage as inflation.

All other allowances have to be claimed on the tax return.

Higher age-related personal allowance

If you are over 65 at the end of the tax year, you can claim the higher age-related personal allowance. In order to do this, you must enter your date of birth on the tax return. There are two rates of higher allowance:

● £5,790 if you are aged between 65 and 74 at the end of the tax year

● £6,050 if you are aged 75 or over at the end of the tax year.

HOW?

To claim the higher age-related allowance, enter your date of birth in box 21.4 on page 7 of your self assessment tax return. See Figure 2.

Restriction of higher age-related allowances

If your annual income is over a certain level, the higher age-related allowance is restricted. For the 2000/2001 tax year, the income level is £16,800 per year. The restriction is that your allowance is reduced by one half of the excess of your income over the limit.

Example
You are aged 65 in the tax year. Your total income for the year is £17,200. The calculation is as follows:

Normal allowance		5,790
Income	17,200	
Restriction level	17,000	
Excess over level	200	
One half excess		100
Restricted allowance		£5,690

The allowance cannot, however, be restricted to an amount less than the normal personal allowance for a person under 65. If the restriction would bring the allowance down to a figure lower than this, the allowance is restricted only as far as the normal personal allowance.

OTHER INFORMATION *for the year ended 5 April 2000*

Q17 Have you already had any 1999-2000 tax refunded or set off by your Inland Revenue office or the Benefits Agency (in Northern Ireland, the Social Security Agency)? *Read the notes on page 26 of your Tax Return Guide*

NO ☐ YES ☐

If yes, enter the amount of the refund in box 17.1.

17.1 £

Q18 Do you want to calculate your tax?

NO ☐ YES ☐

If yes, do it now and then fill in boxes 18.1 to 18.9. Your Tax Calculation Guide will help.

- Unpaid tax for earlier years included in your tax code for 1999-2000
18.1 £

- Tax due for 1999-2000 included in your tax code for a later year
18.2 £

- Total tax and Class 4 NIC due for 1999-2000 **before** you made any payments on account *(put the amount in brackets if an overpayment)*
18.3 £

- Tax due for earlier years
18.4 £

- Tick box 18.5 if you have calculated tax overpaid for earlier years (and enter the amount in the 'Additional information' box on page 8)
18.5 ☐

- Your first payment on account for 2000-2001 *(include the pence)*
18.6 £

Tick box 18.7 if you are making a claim to reduce your 2000-2001 payments on account and say why in the 'Additional information' box
18.7 ☐

Tick box 18.8 if you do **not** need to make 2000-2001 payments on account
18.8 ☐

- Tick box 18.9 if you are reclaiming 2000-2001 tax now (and enter the amount in the 'Additional information' box on page 8)
18.9 ☐

Q19 Do you want to claim a repayment if you have paid too much tax? *(If you tick 'No' or the tax you have overpaid is below £10, I will amount you are owed to reduce your next tax bill.)*

YES ☐

If yes, fill in boxes 19.1A to 19.12 as appropriate

Should the repayment be sent:

- direct to your bank or building society account?
Tick box 19.1A and fill in boxes 19.3 to 19.7
19.1A ☐
or
by cheque to you at your home address
Tick box 19.1B
19.1B ☐

OR

- to a nominee? Tick box 19.2 and fill in boxes 19.3 to 19.12 as appropriate
19.2 ☐

Fill in boxes 19.3 to 19.7 if the repayment is to be sent to your own, or your nominees' bank or building society account

Name of bank or building society 19.3

Branch sort code 19.4 — —

Account number 19.5

Name of account 19.6

Building society ref. 19.7

If your nominee is your agent, *tick box 19.8*
19.8 ☐

Agent's reference for you (if your agent is your nominee)
19.9

Name of your nominee/agent

I authorise 19.10

Nominee/agent address 19.11

Postcode

to receive on my behalf the amount due

This authority must be signed by you. A photocopy of your signature will not do.
19.12

Signature

Q20 Are your details on the front of the Tax Return wrong?

NO ☐ YES ☐

If yes, please make any corrections on the front of the form.

Q21 Please give other personal details in boxes 21.1 to 21.6. *This information helps us to be more efficient and effective and may support claims you have made elsewhere in your Tax Return*

Please give a daytime telephone number if convenient. It is often simpler to phone if we need to ask you about your Tax Return.

Your telephone number 21.1

or, if you prefer, your agent's telephone number 21.2 (also give your agent's name and reference in the 'Additional information' box on page 8)

Enter your first two forenames 21.5

Say if you are single, married, widowed, divorced or separated 21.3

Date of birth 21.4 / /

Enter your date of birth if you are self-employed, or you were born before 6 April 1935, or you have ticked the 'Yes' box in Question 14, or you are claiming relief for Venture Capital Trust subscriptions

Enter your National Insurance number (if known) 21.6

Fig. 2. Page 7 of self assessment tax return.

Example
You are aged 77 in the tax year. Your income is £25,000. The calculation is as follows:

Normal age allowance		6,050
Income	25,000	
Restriction level	17,000	
Excess	8,000	
One half excess		4,000
Restricted allowance		£2,050

But the allowance cannot be restricted below the personal allowance of £4,385.

Marginal rate of tax

It is not hard to see that if you are entitled to a higher age-related allowance, then once your income is above the restriction level, you are paying a higher marginal rate of tax.

Example
You are aged 65, and your total income for the year is £19,500. Compare the tax payable with that payable if your income was £17,000.

Income			19,500
Allowance – normal age allowance		5,790	
Income	19,500		
Restriction level	17,000		
Excess	2,500		
One half excess		1,250	
Restricted allowance			4,540
Taxable			£14,960
Tax 10% on 1520		152.00	
22% on 13,440		2,956.80	
Total		£3,108.80	

Income			17,000
Allowance – age			5,790
Taxable			11,210
Tax 10% on 1,520		152.00	
22% on 9,690		2,131.80	
Total		£2,283.80	

Thus the total tax on income of £19,500 is £3,108.80, and on income of £17,000 it is £2,283.80. There is £825 extra tax to pay on an extra £2,500 income. This means that the top £2,500 of income has suffered tax at 33%.

This concept of 'marginal tax' is one which we shall see again in other guises.

Tax tip
Keep income out of the band that is taxed at a higher rate. Here is one way to do this.

HOW?

Income from an insurance 'bond', if restricted to 5% withdrawals of the amount invested, is not taken into account for tax purposes. The withdrawals up to 5% are effectively accumulated for up to 20 years. Thus, if you had income in, say, a building society account earning interest at 5%, and this took you over the limit for restriction of the higher age-related allowance, you could take the money out and put it in an insurance bond, and still draw the same 5% income. For tax purposes, however, that income would not be taxed, and you would have saved tax at 33% on the income you draw.

Question and answer
Is it worth while reducing my income to keep out of this marginal tax rate?

Never deliberately reduce your income or incur an expense just to save tax. You are still losing out. For example, if you reduced your income to avoid the marginal rate of 33% mentioned above, you would still be worse off to the extent of 67 pence for every pound by which you reduced your income.

Transitional allowance
This is an allowance which was given when separate taxation for married people was introduced in the late 1980s. It relieved a situation where a wife was earning more than her husband. The allowance is gradually dying out, but a few people still claim it. You may claim this allowance if:

- you are a married woman, and

- you had a transitional allowance in the previous tax year, and

- you lived with the same husband in the previous tax year, and

- your husband was resident in the UK for the tax year, and

- your husband has written to his tax district asking for the relief to be given to you.

Higher age-related married couple's allowance

If either spouse is over 65, the married couple's allowance is increased according to the age of the older spouse at the end of the tax year. The allowances are:

- £5,185 if the older spouse is between 65 and 74 at the end of the tax year

- £5,255 if the older spouse is 75 or over at the end of the tax year.

The relief is given at 10%. The higher amount may be claimed by the husband. The wife may claim to have one half of the lower amount of £2,000, or the husband and wife may jointly claim for the wife to have all of the £2,000 allowance. The results are therefore that either:

- the husband receives £5,185 (or £5,255 if 75 or over), or

- the husband receives £3,185 (or £3,255 if 75 or over) and the wife receives £2,000, or

- the husband receives £4,185 (or £4,255 if 75 or over) and the wife receives £1,000.

HOW?

Enter your date of birth in box 21.4 on page 7 and your wife's date of birth in box 16.7 on page 6 of your self assessment tax return.

Restriction of higher married couple's allowance

The higher age-related allowance for married couples is also restricted if the income is over the restriction level (£17,000 for 2000/2001). The restriction is one half of the excess over £17,000, less any restriction already applied to the personal allowance.

The higher marginal rate can therefore also apply due to this restriction.

Blind person's allowance

If you are registered as a blind person during any part of the tax year, you may claim this allowance. For 2000/2001, the allowance is £1,400. This allowance is given at your top rate of tax. It is also transferable between husband and wife. Therefore, if you qualify for the allowance, but do not have enough income to use it, you may transfer it to your spouse.

HOW?

Enter details of your registration in boxes 16.1 to 16.2 on page 6 of your self assessment tax return. See Figure 1.

CAPITAL ALLOWANCES

If you use an asset for your business or your work, you may claim capital allowances as a deduction from your income for tax purposes.

If you use the asset partly for business and partly for private use, the allowance is worked out in the normal way, but only the business proportion is given as a deduction from your income.

A more detailed explanation of the way capital allowances work is provided in Chapter 5.

HOW?

Claim capital allowances by entering the amount in box 1.35 of page 2 of the employment pages (see Figure 3), or boxes 3.61 to 3.70 on page 3 of the self-employment pages (see Figure 4).

Question and answer
What items can I claim capital allowances on?

There is really no restriction on what assets you can claim on. It could be something as small as a hand drill, or as large as an aeroplane. The only test is that it is used for business purposes. If there is any private usage, the proportion of allowances claimable is limited to the business proportion only.

CASE STUDIES

Mary forgets to claim her widow's bereavement allowance

Mary was widowed during the 1999/2000 tax year. She claimed her bereavement allowance for that year, but forgot about it in the

Income from employment continued

■ *Lump sums and compensation payments or benefits including such payments and benefits from a former employer*
Note that 'lump sums' here includes any contributions which your employer made to an unapproved retirement benefits scheme

You must read page EN6 of the Notes **before** filling in boxes 1.24 to 1.30

Reliefs

- £30,000 exemption — **1.24** £
- Foreign service and disability — **1.25** £
- Retirement and death lump sums — **1.26** £

Taxable lump sums

- From box H of *Help Sheet IR204* — **1.27** £
- From box Q of *Help Sheet IR204* — **1.28** £
- From box R of *Help Sheet IR204* — **1.29** £
- Tax deducted from payments in boxes 1.27 to 1.29 — Tax deducted **1.30** £

■ *Foreign earnings not taxable in the UK in year ended 5 April 20   — see   page EN6* — **1.31** £

■ *Expenses you incurred in doing your job - see Notes page   to EN*

- Travel and subsistence costs — **1.32** £
- Fixed deductions for expenses — **1.33** £
- Professional fees and   — **1.34** £
- Other exp   and   allowa   — **1.35** £
- Tick box   fig   n box 1.32 includes travel between your home and a permanent workplace — **1.36**

■ *Foreign Earnings Deduction* — **1.37** £

■ *Foreign tax for which tax credit relief not claimed* — **1.38** £

Additional information

Now fill in any other supplementary Pages that apply to you.
Otherwise, go back to page 2 in your Tax Return and finish filling it in.

Fig. 3. Employment pages of tax return: page 2.

> You must fill in this Page *(leave blank any boxes that do not apply to you)*

Capital allowances - summary

	Capital allowances	Balancing charge
• Motor cars (Separate calculations must be made for each motor car costing more than £12,000 and for cars used partly for private motoring.)	3.61 £	3.62 £
• Other business plant and machinery	3.63 £	3.64 £
• Agricultural or Industrial Buildings Allowance (A separate calculation must be made for each block of expenditure.)	3.65 £	3.66 £
• Other capital allowances claimed (Separate calculations must be made.)	3.67 £	3.68 £
	total of column above	total of column above
Total capital allowances/balancing charges	3.69 £	3.70 £

Adjustments to arrive at taxable profit or loss

Basis period begins 3.71 / / and ends 3.72 / /

- Tick box 3.72A if the figure in box 3.88 is provisional — 3.72A

- Tick box 3.72B if the special arrangements for certain trades detailed in the guidance notes apply (see Notes, pages SEN8 and SEN10) — 3.72B

Profit or loss of this account for tax purposes (box 3.13 or 3.60) — 3.73 £

Adjustment to arrive at profit or loss for this basis period — 3.74 £

- Overlap profit brought forward 3.75 £   Deduct overlap relief used this year 3.76 £

- Overlap profit carried forward

Adjustment for farmers' averaging (see Notes, page SEN8 if you made a loss for 1999-2000) — 3.78 £

Adjustment on change of accounting — 3.78A £

Net profit for 1999-2000 (if loss, enter '0')	3.79 £
Allowable loss for 1999-2000 (if you made a profit, enter '0')	3.80 £
• Loss offset against other income for 1999-2000	3.81 £
• Loss to carry back	3.82 £
• Loss to carry forward (that is allowable loss not claimed in any other way)	3.83 £
• Losses brought forward from earlier years	3.84 £
• Losses brought forward from earlier years used this year	3.85 £

box 3.79 *minus* box 3.85

Taxable profit after losses brought forward — 3.86 £

- Any other business income (for example, Business Start-up Allowance received in 1999-2000) — 3.87 £

box 3.86 + box 3.87

Total taxable profits from this business — 3.88 £

Fig. 4. Self-employed pages of tax return: page 3.

2000/2001 tax year. A friend pointed this out to her, but she had already sent in her tax return for 2000/2001. Fortunately, she does not lose the allowance. She can amend her tax return by writing to the Inspector of Taxes at any time up to 31 January 2003.

David transfers some investments to his wife

David is aged 66, and his total income is £18,200. This puts him into the marginal tax band, as we have seen. This is because his age allowance has been restricted. His income is made up as follows:

| Pension | £12,000 |
| Investment income | £6,200 |

He decides to transfer some of the investments to his wife. This reduces his income by £4,000 and increases his wife's income by £4,000. He has reduced his tax bill by 33% of £4, 000, and his wife has increased her tax bill by only 10% of £4,000 – she is not liable to a higher rate of tax. Between them, they have therefore saved £920.

PERSONAL TAX EFFICIENCY AUDIT

1. Are you sure that you are claiming all the tax allowances that you can?

2. Have you read the notes to the tax return to ensure that you understand all the qualifications for claiming the various allowances?

3. Are you sure that everyone in your family is using all their personal allowances?

3

Paying Less Income Tax – 2

Reliefs are given in a different way from allowances. Generally, they are recognition of payments or expenses of some sort which are allowed as deductions from your income for tax purposes. These reliefs have to be claimed on your tax return. Therefore, make sure you claim all the reliefs to which you are entitled.

HOW?
Claim reliefs by entering the details on page 5 of your self assessment tax return. See Figure 5.

USING YOUR RELIEFS

Pension Contributions
You are allowed to claim relief against your income in respect of premiums you pay towards retirement schemes. However, in order to qualify for the tax relief, the retirement scheme has to be recognised by the Inland Revenue, and the rules of the scheme have to comply with Inland Revenue requirements. These schemes are known as **personal pension schemes**. They replaced retirement annuity schemes in 1988. Both types of scheme provide the same general benefits. Although retirement annuities are no longer available as new contracts, there are many people who still pay premiums under these schemes.

The main purpose of these schemes must be the provision for an individual of a retirement annuity in old age. The most obvious restriction therefore is in taking benefits.

Benefits may not be taken before the age of 50 for personal pension schemes and 60 for retirement annuity schemes. However, there are lower age limits for certain occupations, such as downhill skiers, athletes or sportsmen, divers, dancers, trapeze artists, etc.

The main tax advantages in these schemes is that tax relief is given on premiums paid, and this tax relief is available at your highest marginal rate of tax. When you take the benefits, a certain amount (up

RELIEFS *for the year ended 5 April 2000*

Q14 **Do you want to claim relief for pension contributions?** **NO** **YES** If yes, fill in boxes 14.1 to 14.17 as appropriate

*Do not include contributions deducted from your pay by your employer to their pension scheme, because tax relief is given automatically. But **do include** your contributions to personal pension schemes and free-standing AVC schemes.*

■ *Retirement annuity contracts*

| Qualifying payments made in 1999-2000 | **14.1** £ | 1999-2000 payments used in an earlier year | **14.2** £ | Relief claimed |
| 1999-2000 payments now to be carried back | **14.3** £ | Payments brought back from 2000-2001 | **14.4** £ | box 14.1 *minus* (boxes 14.2 and 14.3, but not 14.4) **14.5** £ |

■ *Self-employed contributions to personal pension plans*

| Qualifying payments made in 1999-2000 | **14.6** £ | 1999-2000 payments used in an earlier year | **14.7** £ | Relief claimed |
| 1999-2000 payments now to be carried back | **14.8** £ | Payments brought back from 2000-2001 | **14.9** £ | box 14.6 *minus* (boxes 14.7 and 14.8, but not 14.9) **14.10** £ |

■ *Employee contributions to personal pension plans (include your gross contribution - see the note on box 14.11 in your Tax Return Guide)*

| Qualifying payments made in 1999-2000 | **14.11** £ | 1999-2000 payments used in an earlier year | **14.12** £ | Relief claimed |
| 1999-2000 payments now to be carried back | **14.13** £ | Payments brought back from 2000-2001 | £ | box 14.11 *minus* (boxes 14.12 and 14.13, but not 14.14) **14.15** £ |

■ *Contributions to other pension schemes and free-standing AVC schemes*

● Amount of contributions to employer's schemes **not deducted** from your pay **14.16** £

● Gross amount of free-standing additional voluntary contributions paid in 1999-2000 **14.17** £

Q15 **Do you want to claim any of these following reliefs?** **NO** **YES** If yes, fill in boxes 15.1 to 15.12, as appropriate.

● Payments you made to a vocational training (read the box 15.1 note on page 20 of your Tax Return Guide) | Amount of payment **15.1** £

● Interest eligible for relief on loans to buy your main home (other than MIRAS) | Amount of payment **15.2** £

● Interest eligible for relief on other qualifying loans | Amount of payment **15.3** £

● Maintenance or alimony payments you have made under a court order, Child Support Agency assessment or legally binding order or agreement | Amount claimed under 'new' rules **15.4** £

| Amount claimed under 'old' rules up to £1,970 **15.5** £ | Amount claimed under 'old' rules over £1,970 **15.6** £ |

● Subscriptions for Venture Capital Trust shares (up to £100,000) | Amount on which relief claimed **15.7** £

● Subscriptions under the Enterprise Investment Scheme (up to £150,000) | Amount on which relief claimed **15.8** £

● Charitable covenants or annuities | Amount of payment **15.9** £

● Gift Aid and Millennium Gift Aid | Amount of qualifying payments **15.10** £

● Post-cessation expenses, pre-incorporation losses brought forward and losses on relevant discounted securities, etc. | Amount of payment **15.11** £

● Payments to a trade union or friendly society for death benefits | Half amount of payment **15.12** £

SPECIMEN

Fig. 5. Page 5 of self assessment tax return.

to 25% of the fund in the case of personal pension schemes) may be taken as a tax-free lump sum.

Relevant income
You may claim this relief if you have relevant income. Basically this includes earned income – either self-employed, or employed. If you are employed, you are only eligible if the earnings are non-pensionable, i.e. the employer does not have a superannuation scheme. Included in the definition of earned income for these purposes is income from furnished holiday lettings.

Contributions limits
You may claim relief for contributions to these schemes up to certain limits. The limits are related to your age at the end of the tax year, and the amount of relevant income. These limits are as follows, expressed as a percentage of net relevant income:

	Personal pensions	*Retirement annuities*
Age at beginning of tax year	%	%
Up to 35	17.5	17.5
36 to 45	20	17.5
46 to 50	25	17.5
51 to 55	30	20
56 to 60	35	22.5
61 or more	40	27.5

If you pay premiums under both types of schemes, the limit for retirement annuities is applied first, then any surplus is allowed under personal pension limits.

There is an overall limit to the premiums you may pay in any one tax year. For the 2000/2001 tax year, any relevant earnings over £91,800 are disregarded. The maximum you could pay is therefore 40% of £91,800, if you are 61 or over at the beginning of the tax year.

HOW?
Enter details in boxes 14.1 to 14.17 on page 5 of your self assessment tax return. See Figure 5.

Carry back of premiums

You may also elect that the premiums you pay in one tax year be 'carried back' to the previous tax year and tax relief is given on the previous year's figures. This could be useful where:

● you could not afford to pay the premiums in one tax year, or

● you paid tax at a higher rate in the earlier year, or

● rates of tax generally were higher in the previous year.

Carry forward of unused relief

If you did not use your maximum relief in any one tax year, the unused relief is available as a 'carry forward' for up to six years. In order to use this relief brought forward from an earlier year, you must have used up all the current year's relief first.

Examples

● Carry back of premium

You are aged 44, and self-employed. Your business made an abnormally large profit of £50,000 taxable in 1999/2000. You paid only £500 in pension premiums in the 1999/2000 tax year. The maximum pension premiums on which you can claim tax relief for the year is 20% of £50,000, i.e. £10,000. Therefore, as you only paid £500 in 1999/2000, you may then pay up to £9,500 in 2000/2001, and claim for it to be carried back to 1999/2000. You would get tax relief at your top rate of tax for 1999/2000, which would have been 40%.

● Carry forward of unused relief

Assume the same circumstances as in the above example. In addition, the profits and pension premiums for earlier years were as follows:

	Profits	Pension premiums	Relief available	Unused relief
1995/96	15,000	500	3,000	2,500
1996/97	15,000	500	3,000	2,500
1997/98	20,000	500	4,000	3,500
1998/99	18,000	500	3,600	3,100
Total unused relief				£11,600

After the maximum 1999/2000 relief of £10,000 has been paid, up to a further £11,600 may be paid and claimed by using up the unused relief brought forward.

Timing the relief

As we have seen, the relief is given at your highest marginal rate of tax. The best strategy for claiming the relief is therefore to claim it when you are paying the highest rate of tax. In the examples above, the abnormally large profit taxed in 1999/2000 caused the tax rate to go up to 40%. Paying premiums in the same year or the following year allowed maximum use to be made of the carry back and carry forward rules.

This principle could also be used when the standard tax rate goes down. For example, in 1999/2000 the standard rate of tax was 23%, but it is 22% in 2000/2001. The effect is not as great as the decrease from the higher rate of tax to the standard rate, of course, but it can contribute towards saving tax.

Question and answer
How much should I put into a pension policy?

There can be no definitive answer. Everything depends upon your circumstances. The table on page 28 shows the maximum you can contribute to get tax relief. But other circumstances will come into play. For instance, your age will play a large part. The nearer we get to retirement, the greater our concern that we are adequately provided for. If you are employed, obviously an employer's contributory scheme will be much more valuable, whatever your age.

On the whole, my advice is to pay as much as you can comfortably afford.

Vocational training payments

Payments for the training costs of a qualifying course are eligible for tax relief. A qualifying course is one that counts towards accreditation as a National or Scottish Vocational Qualification. If you are registered for a course, the course provider will know if it qualifies for tax relief, and the fees you pay will be after tax relief.

HOW?
Enter details in box 15.1 on page 5 of your self assessment tax return. See Figure 5.

Interest on loans – MIRAS

Interest on a mortgage for buying a house attracts tax relief until 5th April 2000 within certain limits. The limits are as follows:

● Tax relief is given at 10% only.

● Tax relief is given on a maximum loan of £30,000 only. If the loan is greater than this, then the interest is apportioned, and tax relief given on interest on the first £30,000 only.

● Tax relief is only given on interest on a loan for buying a house which is your only or main residence – not for a loan for improving a house, or for buying a second home.

● If more than one person is buying the house, there is only one £30,000 limit, which the joint owners must apportion between them.

● Tax relief is given at source. That is to say that you pay to the bank or building society only the net amount after tax relief has been deducted. The bank or building society then reclaim the tax from the Inland Revenue.

HOW?
This relief is given at source. You do not have to claim it in your tax return.

Interest on loans – other
There is tax relief on interest on some other loans, as follows:

● If you borrow money to buy a house from someone other than an authorised lender (such as a bank or building society), they are not able to operate the MIRAS system. You can then claim the 10% tax relief on the interest you pay, with the same limitations as for MIRAS. This relief ceased on 5 April 2000.

HOW?
Claim it in box 15.2 on page 5 of your self assessment tax return. See Figure 5.

● You can claim tax relief at your highest marginal rate of tax on interest on the following types of loans:
  – A loan to invest money in a partnership in which you are a partner, or in a limited company in which you are a director.
  – A loan to buy land or property which is used by a partnership in which you are a partner.

- A loan to buy plant or machinery for use in a business of a partnership in which you are a partner.
- A loan to pay inheritance tax.

HOW?
Enter details in box 15.3 on page 5 of your self assessment tax return. See Figure 5.

Maintenance or alimony

Tax relief can be claimed on certain payments of maintenance or alimony since 14 March 1988. The payments must be made under a Court Order or a written agreement under an assessment made under the Child Support Act 1991. The tax relief is the lower of:

- the amount of maintenance or alimony paid, and
- the married couple's tax allowance for the year. From 6 April 2000, use the figure of £2,000.

HOW?
Enter details in boxes 15.4 to 15.6 on page 5 of your self assessment tax return. See Figure 5.

Venture capital trusts

These are investments in businesses not quoted on the Stock Exchange, which meet certain criteria. Investments up to £100,000 attract tax relief of 20%.

HOW?
Enter details in box 15.7 on page 5 of your self assessment tax return. See Figure 5.

Enterprise investment scheme

The Enterprise Investment Scheme is similar to the Venture Capital Trusts. Tax relief at 20% is given on investments in shares in qualifying companies, with an upper limit of £100,000.

HOW?
Enter details in box 15.8 on page 5 of your self assessment tax return. See Figure 5.

Charitable covenants

If you donate to a registered charity under a deed of covenant which lasts at least four years, the amount you pay is deemed to be net of basic rate income tax. The charity can claim back the deemed tax. For your own tax purposes, the 'grossed up' amount is added to your income, but is then also deducted as an annual payment, and effectively relieved at your highest marginal rate of tax.

A deed of covenant is merely a promise to pay the amount involved for the period of time stated. However, it is enforceable under law. This means that if you did not complete your payments, the charity could, if they chose to, sue you for the rest of the money promised.

Example

You pay a charitable covenant of £780 a year. You are deemed to have paid £1,000 and deducted tax at 22% (£220). The charity claims back the £220. If your total income was £36,000, the tax situation would be as follows:

Total income		36,000
Covenant deducted		1,000
Net income		35,000
Personal allowance		4,385
Taxable		30,615
Tax due	10% on 1,520	152.00
	22% on 26,880	5,913.60
	40% on 2,215	886.00
		6,951.60
Add tax deducted from covenant		220.00
Total tax		£7,171.60

Thus, the tax on the 'top slice' of £1,000 income has been taxed at only 22%, instead of 40%.

HOW?

Enter details in box 15.9 on page 5 of your self assessment tax return. See Figure 5

Gift aid

If you make any payment to a registered charity, you may sign a gift aid form, which the charity can provide, and the amount is deemed to be net of basic rate income tax. The charity can then claim back the deemed tax. The limit for the 'Millennium gift aid' scheme is £100. This scheme is to encourage gifts to charities providing help to underdeveloped countries and donations must be made by 31 December 2000.

HOW?

Enter details in box 15.10 on page 5 of your self assessment tax return. See Figure 5.

CASE STUDY

Stan pays a lump sum 'single premium' pension

Stan, self-employed, has had a windfall, and puts some of it in a building society account. He decides he wants to improve his pension by putting as much as he can into a pension plan. He works out:

● the maximum he can contribute this year, and

● the maximum unused allowances that can be brought forward.

The total comes to £15,000.

He then consults an independent financial advisor and decides to split the amount in two. He puts half in a single premium policy which is unit linked, and the other half in a single premium policy which is 'with profits'.

He gets tax relief on all the premium he pays, some at his top tax rate of 40%.

PERSONAL TAX EFFICIENCY AUDIT

1. How are you funding your retirement? Are you taking as much advantage of tax reliefs as you can?

2. Are you borrowing money in the most tax-efficient way?

3. If you give to charities, are you doing it in a tax-efficient way?

4

Paying Less Income Tax – 3

If you have control over your income, or some parts of it, you may be able to control the timing of receipt of the income. This could be useful in saving tax. There may, for instance, be occasions when you know you will be paying less tax one year than in the following or the preceding year. The tax rates and the personal allowances usually alter from one year to another, and it may be useful to have income in a later year to benefit from the higher allowances or lower rates of tax in that year.

Another scenario in which your tax liability could change drastically from one year to the next is on retirement. You could well be paying the top rate of tax the year before you retire, then the standard or even the lower rate after you retire. This could be partly due to the drop in your income, and partly due to the extra tax allowance on reaching the age of 65. There is a further increase in the allowance (though not so great) on reaching age 75.

Another reason for postponing income from one year to the next is that there is a further year in which to pay the tax. For instance, income received on 5 April 2000 will be liable for tax on 31 January 2001. Income received on 6 April 2000 will be liable for tax on 31 January 2002.

TIMING YOUR TRANSACTIONS

Bringing income forward

HOW?

If you want to have income taxed in the current year instead of the next tax year, and you have a bank or building society account, or some other form of money on deposit, you could close the account.

This could help if the interest would have been payable in, say, June. By closing the account in March, the interest is then paid up to the date of closing the account, and therefore comes before 5 April. Of course, you must be certain that there is no penalty on closing the account, and that you can get at least as good an interest rate in a new account.

Postponing income

HOW?

You may also be able to use a bank or building society account to postpone income. This is only possible where the right sort of account exists. There are accounts which are long-term accounts (such as five years) and only pay interest at the end of the five years. Some such accounts are promoted by some building societies in the form of 'Stockmarket Bonds'. They guarantee to pay an interest rate which at least matches the increase in the stockmarket index over a five-year period. The interest for the whole five years is then paid at the end of the term. This does produce a 'bunching' of five years' interest all receivable in one year, but it does also postpone income.

Controlling payment dates

We have also seen in the previous chapter how to use pension premiums as a relief from income tax. We have seen how they can be backdated to the previous year, and how unused relief can be carried forward up to six years. Because this relief is dependent on when you pay the premiums, you have total control over this aspect of your tax affairs. A good principle, therefore, is to pay more premiums when you have a greater tax liability, particularly if you are liable to tax at the higher rate.

Accrued income

Certain fixed interest securities, such as government stocks, pay interest half yearly. If you buy or sell them on the stockmarket, there is an adjustment made on the price to account for interest accrued from the last interest payment. Thus, if you are buying, you have to pay extra for the interest accrued since the last payment. This is because you will receive the whole of the next half-yearly interest payment. It works the opposite way round if you are selling.

Thus, you can either be paying for accrued interest, or receiving accrued interest. If you receive it, it is taxable, and if you pay it, you can deduct it from the interest you receive. This arrangement does allow a certain amount of flexibility in timing the transactions.

It could put income into a different tax year. However, you must bear in mind that doing this will incur dealing costs. It is therefore not something to be recommended to carry out on a regular basis, but something to bear in mind as a one-off way of influencing the timing of income.

This is a general principle, since the opportunities to save tax by timing tend to occur infrequently. We have already seen the sort of occasions on which this can be useful, such as:

● retirement

● attaining the age of 65 or 75

● receiving an abnormal income or profit which puts you in the higher-rate tax band for one year only.

Question and answer
I expect my business to take off next year, and earn really big profits. Should I put off paying a pension premium so that I can claim it later when I expect to be in a higher-rate tax band?

It all depends on how concrete your expectations are. We all tend to be over-optimistic about our future business prospects. I would caution against putting off pension premiums for too long. The effect of postponing premiums to a pension policy can be far more drastic to the end result than the tax benefit. If there is any doubt, continue to pay a modest amount now – one that you can comfortably afford. Then put in more when your business does better and you can better afford extra premiums.

USING YOUR LOWER-RATE BANDS

You can look on your lower-rate tax bands as a sort of allowance. As we saw in Chapter 2, if you are married and have some control over income, you can ensure that allowances are fully used up. You can also make sure that the lower-rate bands are used up as much as possible.

For instance, if the husband is taxable at 40%, but the wife is only taxable at 10%, it would make sense to transfer some of the income to the wife and thereby save 30% on the income transferred. The same is true, of course, if one partner is taxable at 40% and the other at 22%, or one at 22% and the other at 10%.

Example

Mr and Mrs Jones have the following income and tax liability:

		Husband	*Wife*
Salary		35,000	5,000
Interest		3,000	1,000
Total income		38,000	6,000
Personal allowance		4,385	4,385
Taxable		33,615	1,615
Tax due	10% on 1,520	152.00	
	22% on 26,880	5,913.60	
	40% on 5,215	2,086.00	
	10% on 1,615		161.50
Total tax		8,151.60	161.50

The total tax paid between them is £8,313.10.

If they transferred the source of interest from the husband to the wife, the result would be:

Salary		35,000	5,000
Interest			4,000
Total income		35,000	9,000
Personal allowance		4,385	4,385
Taxable		30,615	4,615
Tax due	10% on 1,520	152.00	860
	22% on 26,880	5,913.60	
	40% on 2,215	886.00	
	10% on 1,520		152
	20% on 3,095		619
(investment income)		£6,799.60	£771.00

The total tax paid between them is £7,570.60

There has been a saving of £742.50, by using up the wife's lower-rate tax band and investment tax band to the full.

HOW?

Use up lower-rate bands by ensuring that income is divided between husband and wife in the right proportions. It is simple to transfer a building society account or bank account to your spouse's name. He or she opens up a new account, and you withdraw the right amount and give it to him or her. Shares or unit trusts can be transferred by writing to the company or unit trust manager. They will send you transfer forms to sign.

EXTRA STATUTORY CONCESSIONS AND SPECIAL CASES

The Inland Revenue publish concessions. These are treatments of certain items for tax purposes which are not laid down by law, but allowed by the Inland Revenue. They are all treatments which benefit the taxpayer. The list is long, and it is not possible to give it in full here, but here are some of the concessions which you may find useful:

● **Flat-rate expenses** for tools, clothing, etc. These are allowances agreed for employees in various trades or industry groups. They are usually agreed with the relevant trade unions. Check with your union or employer to see if there is a claim you can make.

HOW?

Find out the amount and enter it in your self assessment tax return box 1.33 on page 2 of the employment pages. See Figure 3.

● **Luncheon vouchers** given by employers are not taxable up to certain limits.

● **Travel expenses** from home to work are not normally allowable against tax. But if an employer reimburses travel costs for home-to-work travel, that can be free of tax if it is as a result of public transport disruption due to industrial action, or if an employee is severely disabled and therefore unable to use public transport.

● **Arrears of tax** due to official error. If the Inland Revenue have not charged you to tax, even though you have given them all the information, and then they charge you late, you may apply for some or all of the tax to be remitted. The level of remission depends on your total income in the year of notification of the tax arrears, as follows:

Taxpayer's gross income   *Tax remitted*

– up to £15,500   All
– £15,501 to £18,000   Three quarters
– £18,001 to £22,000   One half
– £22,001 to £26,000   One quarter
– £26,001 to £40,000   One tenth
– over £40,000   None

HOW?

If you have been in these circumstances, make sure you claim the exemption by demanding it from your tax inspector.

● If your employer has a **suggestions scheme** to which all employees are able to contribute, and you gain an award (up to £5,000), it is not taxable by concession.

● **Long-service awards** of tangible goods, or shares in the employer company to people who have served for at least 20 years with the same employer, are not taxable by concession provided that the cost to the employer does not exceed £20 for each year of service, and no similar award has been made in the previous ten years to the same person.

● **Capital allowances:** if you cease trading, you may use capital allowances brought forward to reduce the profit or create a loss for the final year's assessment.

● **Overseas employment:** certain lump sums from termination of overseas employment may not be taxable.

GETTING THE RIGHT KIND OF TAX CREDITS

From 6 April 1999, dividends from companies have carried a tax credit of 10% (previously the figure was 20%). Further, this tax credit is not repayable. It was always repayable in the past.

Taxpayers who pay tax at either the lower rate or the basic rate will incur no further liability. Higher-rate taxpayers will be liable to the extra tax charge for the higher rate.

However, those who would otherwise have been due for a repayment, because their personal allowances have not been fully used, will not be able to reclaim the tax credit on dividends. If you are in this position, you should think about changing your investment from shares which attract dividends to interest which is either paid gross, or with tax deducted at source. This tax deducted at source will still be repayable.

Before you resort to this, however, stop to think about your investment objectives, and whether a change from shares to interest-bearing loans will continue to meet those objectives.

GETTING TAX RELIEF ON YOUR TRAVELLING EXPENSES

If you are employed, the normal rule about tax relief on travel expenses is that home-to-work travel (what we shall call 'commuting') is not allowable. However, this applies to travel between your home and your permanent workplace. A 'permanent workplace' is one which the employee *expects* to attend regularly:

● for more than 24 months, or

● for the whole period he or she holds that particular employment.

Note the word in italics. It is very important.

Certain employees, in particular site based employees, do not fit into this pattern. Their workplace shifts as the employer's work demands alter. This is most common for building site employees, and computer programmers or analysts, who frequently get sent to different locations for their work.

If you are in this position, and you are working at different sites for 24 months or less, then make sure you claim your travel expenses.

There is another twist to the claim, however. This concerns the word *expects* above. If you have an assignment which you expect to last less than two years, you can claim your travel expenses. However, if you are then informed, say, 20 months into the assignment, that your assignment is to be extended, your expectation is now that the assignment will last more than 24 months, so you are not eligible any more to claim travel expenses.

Not all assignments fit neatly into this pattern, however. Your job might entail going to a main office or factory most of the time, and spending a few days a month at another location. It is possible under the rules to have more than one permanent workplace. However, a workplace is not permanent if:

- the assignment there does not last more than 24 months, or

- it takes less than 40% of the employee's working time.

Tax tip

Therefore, if you are in any borderline case, try to arrange with your employer that the assignment will be either:

- 24 months or less, or

- less than 40% of your total working time.

HOW?

You will have to be dependent on your employer for this scheme. It is better to have the term written into a contract. It is possible that the Inspector of Taxes would challenge this, and any form of written evidence will help your case. Claim the expenses by completing box 1.32 on page 2 of the employment pages of your self assessment tax return. See Figure 3.

If you are an employer, you could try to arrange this for your employees, and make sure they are aware they can claim their travel expenses. They will probably be very happy about it.

SAVING TAX ON CAR BENEFIT

If you have the use of a company car, you are charged to tax on the 'basic cash equivalent', which is:

- the cost of the car (i.e. the manufacturer's list price) plus accessories (except any accessories designed for use by disabled people), less

- any capital contributions towards the cost made by the employee.

If the car is a 'classic car' (i.e. over 15 years old and with a market value of over £15,000), then the market value is used instead of the cost.

There is an upper limit of £80,000 on the cost, and an upper limit of £5,000 on the contribution made by the employee.

The amount you are charged is tax on 35% of the 'basic cash equivalent', but this sum is then subject to various reductions, in the following order:

1. according to the business mileage that you do in the car

2. according to the age of the car

3. according to the amount of time the car is available for use, and

4. if the employee has made any contributions for private use.

The figures are as follows:

● Business mileage

  – More than 2,500 miles but less than 18,000 miles: one third reduction.
  – Over 18,000 miles: two thirds reduction.
  – If there is a second company car, there is no reduction for business mileage under 18,000 miles. The reduction for over 18,000 miles is one third. If there are two company cars, the one with the greater business mileage is always the first company car.

● Age of the car: if four years old or more at the end of the tax year, one third reduction.

● Availability during the year: *pro rata* for the amount of time not available.

● For contributions by the employee: pound for pound reduction.

Example
You had a new company car of which the list price was £18,000. This is your 'basic cash equivalent'. The tax is charged on 35% of this figure, i.e. £6,300.

If you did, say, 3,000 business miles, the £6,300 is reduced by one third, i.e. £2,100, leaving £4,200 chargeable to tax.

If you did 20,000 business miles, the £6,300 is reduced by two thirds, i.e. £4,200, leaving £2,100 chargeable to tax.

If you still had the car after four years, and you still did 20,000 business miles, the £2,100 would be reduced by a further one third, i.e. by £700, leaving £1,400 chargeable to tax.

If you made contributions of £50 per month (i.e. £600 per year) for the use of the car, that £1,400 would be reduced to £800.

Tax tip
Keep a regular check on your mileage. You might be in a marginal position of having business mileage just below the threshold for a further reduction. If, for instance, in the middle of March, you have done 17,200 miles, you would do well to try to arrange your schedule so that

you actually do the extra 801 miles needed to qualify for the top band of reduction. This may, of course, need your employer's guidance or co-operation.

Warning

The *pro rata* mileage requirement applies for each period that a particular car is available to you. Therefore, if you change cars during the year, each car is treated separately.

Example

You had a company car until 5 August, and did 5,000 business miles in it. It was then changed for a new car, and in the rest of the tax year you did 15,000 business miles.

At first sight, it appears that you have done 20,000 business miles in total, so you should qualify for the two-thirds reduction. However, each car must be considered individually. Therefore, in the first car, you did 5,000 business miles in four months. The *pro rata* mileage to qualify for the two-thirds reduction is one third of 18,000 i.e. 6,000 miles. Therefore, you would only get a one-third reduction for the first four months. You would, however, qualify for the two-thirds reduction for the other eight months of the year, since your mileage for those eight months was more than the *pro rata* amount (i.e. 12,000 miles).

Therefore, if you know that a car change is approaching, and you are in a marginal position, try to make sure that your business miles are enough.

Tax tip

The rule about capital contributions to the cost of the car by an employee does, of course, mean that, if you make a contribution as an outright payment, the cost of the car is reduced for these purposes. However, it could also apply to a situation where you make a contribution which is partly refundable, when the car is sold. This may, for instance, be a refund related to the number of years you have had the use of the car, or related to the price obtained when your employer sold the car. You still qualify for the reduction (up to the £5,000 limit) even though you later get part of the contribution back.

The Inland Revenue have, however, indicated that the reduction would not apply when the whole of the contribution is refundable. This remains a point to be tested in the courts, however, since the Inland Revenue's statement does not appear to be backed up by any statutory authority.

Another tax tip

The law governing the benefit charged to tax for use of a company car says that the charge shall apply where 'a car is made available without any transfer of the property in it'. Therefore, current thinking is that it may be possible to reduce the tax charge if the employer agrees to a 'shared ownership' plan. Under such a plan, the company could sell a proportion of the ownership of the car to the employee – say, 5%. The employee would, of course, suffer 5% of the depreciation in value when the car was sold, but this could prove a small price to pay for the sake of the tax benefit.

So what would the tax benefit be under this scheme? If the special rules for the tax charge on the benefit of car use do not apply, then the general rules for benefit in kind apply. We have already seen (above) the way the car benefit is charged. The general rules are a little different. The benefit under general rules is as follows:

● 20% of the market value of the item provided for private use (when it is first provided), and

● all of the expenses incurred in the provision of an asset.

The benefit is then apportioned according to the relative amounts of business use and private use.

The key differences are in the percentage charge, the apportionment between business and private use, and the charge for expenses (*ie* running costs). The effect this has on the charge depends on the amount of business mileage and the relative proportion of private mileage.

Example

You are provided with a new company car which cost £20,000. Your business mileage is 6,000, and your private mileage is also 6,000. The annual running costs are £1,000. You have accepted your employer's offer to buy a 5% stake in the car for £1,000. The comparative costs are:

Company car charge to tax:	
Cost (£20,000 less £1,000) x 35%	£6,650
Less one third for mileage	£2,217
Net charge	£4,433

Note that there is no difference whatever the private mileage is. This charge relates to business miles only.

General benefit rules:

Cost (£20,000 less £1,000) x 20%		£3,800
Less one half business use		£1,900
		£1,900
Running costs	£1,000	
Less one half business use	£500	
		£500
Total charge		£2,400

There has been a saving on tax of just over £2,000. If you pay tax at 40%, this would be a real benefit to you of just over £800. Further, this benefit would continue each year. However, the comparison would be different in other circumstances. In particular, the benefit would be greater when:

● the business mileage is low – particularly when it is below 2,500 miles

● there is a second company car

● the private mileage is low compared with the business mileage

● the car is relatively new.

The benefit will be less when:

● the business mileage is high, particularly when it is above 18,000 miles

● there is only one company car

● the private mileage is high compared with the business mileage

● the car is older – particularly when it is four years old or more.

This plan has not yet been challenged in the courts, nor indeed has it been tested out to any great extent.

HOW?
Your employer will have some means of checking the business mileage that you do – based on the records you keep. After the end of the tax year, the employer will issue you with a copy of the P11D return he has made relating to you. You should then enter these amounts on page 1 of the employment pages with your self assessment tax return. See Figure 6.

Income for the year ended 5 April 2000

Inland Revenue

EMPLOYMENT

If you have answered 'Yes' to Question 1, fill in Pages E1 and E2. If you want help, look up the box numbers in the Notes on Employment at the back of your Tax Return Guide. They are colour-coded to match the form. If you are a minister of religion, fill in the Ministers of Religion Pages.

Fill in a separate copy of these Pages for each employment from which you received any income.

Details of employer

Employer's PAYE reference - may be shown under 'Tax Office number and reference' on your P60 or 'PAYE reference' on your P45

1.1

Employer's name

1.2

Date employment started
(only if between 6 April 1999 and 5 April 2000)

1.3 / /

Employer's address

1.5

Date finished (only if between 6 April 1999 and 5 April 2000)

1.4 / /

Tick box 1.6 if you were a director of the company

1.6

and, if so, tick box 1.7 if it was a close company

1.7

stcode

Income from employment

■ *Money - see Notes, page EN3*

● Payments from P60 (or P45 or payslips)

Before tax

1.8 £

● Payments not on P60 etc.   ...ps

1.9 £

...her ...ayments (excluding expenses entered below and lump sums ...mpensation payments or benefits entered overleaf)

1.10 £

● UK tax d...   ...m...   ...ments in boxes 1.8 to 1.10

Tax deducted

1.11 £

SPECIMEN

■ *Benefits and expenses - see Notes, pages EN3 to EN6. If any benefits connected with termination of employment were received, or enjoyed, after that termination and were from a* **former** *employer you need to complete Help Sheet IR204, available from the Orderline. Do not enter such benefits here.*

● Assets transferred/ payments made for you

Amount

1.12 £

● Vans

Amount

1.18 £

● Vouchers/credit cards

Amount

1.13 £

● Interest-free and low-interest loans

Amount

1.19 £

● Living accommodation

Amount

1.14 £

box 1.20 is not used

● Mileage allowance

Amount

1.15 £

● Private medical or dental insurance

Amount

1.21 £

● Company cars

1.16 £

● Other benefits

Amount

1.22 £

● Fuel for company cars

Amount

1.17 £

● Expenses payments received and balancing charges

Amount

1.23 £

Fig. 6. Employment pages of tax return: page 1.

USING ELECTRONIC FILING

If you take advantage of the newly-introduced facility to file your self assessment tax return and pay your tax electronically, you will receive a one-off discount of £10.

CASE STUDIES

Derek postpones some of his income

Derek is retiring in three years' time. He is now in the top tax bracket paying 40% tax. He knows that he will not be in that bracket when he retires. He therefore invests in a building society 'Stockmarket Bond' by which all income will accrue on the fifth anniversary of the bond. He does this by transferring some of the money at present in an ordinary savings account.

Frank gets relief on his travel expenses

Frank is employed as a computer programmer, and does most of his work on premises of his employer's clients. All his assignments last less than 24 months, and he claims travel expenses. However, his employer now approaches him to work on a longer-term contract, which he expects to last more than 24 months. As Frank knows this will disbar him from claiming expenses, he points this out to his employer, and uses it as a bargaining tool to negotiate a better rate of pay for this new assignment.

PERSONAL TAX EFFICIENCY AUDIT

1. Do you know if and when any changes are likely to occur in your circumstances (e.g. retirement, promotion, etc.), leading to a change in your tax rate?

2. Do all your family use up all their lower-rate tax bands? If not, what can you do about it?

3. Have you a clear enough investment policy to decide whether you want interest with tax deducted or dividends with a tax credit?

4. Are your terms of employment adequately defined in your contract of employment?

5. Is your employer willing to co-operate in any scheme you may put to him or her?

5

Paying Less Business Tax – 1

To tax and to please, no more than to love
and be wise, is not given to men.

Edmund Burke

Strictly, there is not a separate tax known as 'business tax'. The tax you pay on your business depends on the format in which you carry on your business. The right format for you depends on your circumstances.

Basically, the choices are as follows:

- limited company
- partnership
- sole trader.

CHOOSING THE RIGHT FORMAT FOR YOUR BUSINESS

Limited company

This means that the limited company is the actual owner of the business. The ownership of the company depends on who holds the shares. It is possible for there to be just one shareholder, but this is not recommended. Shareholdings in the company are also a good way to pass on ownership of the company – say, to the next generation of your family. The company has a separate legal existence to its shareholders, and is a method of protecting them – their liability is limited to the money they put into the business. A limited company must also have at least one director and one secretary. Again, it is recommended that there are always at least two directors.

Limited companies are liable to **corporation tax**. This is charged at the following rates:

Up to £10,000	10%
from £50,001 to £300,000	20%
Above £1,500,000	30%

In the 'gaps' between £10,001 and £50,000, and between £300,001 and £1,500,000, sliding scales operate to gradually increase the rates to the next bands.

Partnership

This consists of two or more people carrying on a business together. The terms of their partnership are governed by a **partnership agreement,** or if there is no partnership agreement, by the Partnership Act 1890.

Each partner is charged to income tax and class 4 National Insurance on their share of profits of the partnership for each tax year. You can be flexible about the way in which profits are shared between the partners, and this can produce savings on the total tax bill. It is often useful to be able to do this where a husband and wife are carrying out a business together.

Sole trader

This is the simplest form of carrying out a business. It simply consists of a person doing business on his or her own account. The person is charged to income tax and class 4 National Insurance on the business profits each year. A person can employ their husband or wife in their business, and pay them a salary. This will use up personal allowances, but the salary must actually be justified by the amount of work done. The salary must also be actually paid and recorded. It cannot be simply a book entry.

The decision whether to employ your spouse or be in partnership with him or her is one which depends on various circumstances – many of which are probably nothing to do with saving tax. However, all other things being equal, it is usually better and more flexible to be in partnership.

Question and answer
Do I have complete freedom to choose in which format my business trades?

Yes, the choice is yours. There may be decision points in your business career when you have to think hard about it. For instance, you may be trading sole, and employing your wife or one of your children. The time may come when you have to think about taking them in to partnership. There may also be external pressures. In some industries, for example, people who can award you a contract may refuse to do so unless you are a limited company.

DECIDING TO GO LIMITED

Before deciding whether your business should be in the format of a limited company or not, there are several matters to consider.

Transferring an existing business

If you are considering making an existing business into a limited company, you need to think about the actual transfer. The limited company must buy the assets from you, the existing trader. This could give rise to a capital gains tax liability. However, if the transfer is handled correctly, this can be deferred. The solution is to issue shares in the new company as the consideration for the assets of the business bought. This effectively defers the capital gains tax liability until the shares are eventually sold. By that time, you may well qualify for retirement relief or tapering relief. There are three conditions which must be met:

1. The whole of the assets of the business must be transferred to the company.

2. The business must be transferred as a going concern.

3. The business must be transferred wholly or partly in exchange for shares issued by the company to the person(s) transferring the business.

However, when transferring a business to a limited company, remember that **stamp duty** is payable on the value of certain assets such as land, goodwill, debtors, etc.

HOW?

To transfer a business from yourself to a limited company, you will probably need the help of a solicitor and/or an accountant. A contract should be drawn up encompassing the above points in the right form. A limited company needs to be formed. There are many company registration agents who can register a company for you – either tailored to your specific requirements or an 'off the shelf' company. The date of registration of the company is not necessarily the same date as the start of trading of the business in its new format. That comes once the sale contract is agreed.

Tax tip

If you transfer a business from yourself to a limited company which you control, the Inland Revenue consider this as a transaction between connected persons. They will then seek to impose a market value on all trading stock which is transferred to the company. This will have the effect of making you taxable on the full selling price of trading stock before you have actually sold it. This could be especially costly where there is a large difference between the cost of the stock and the full selling price. A particular example of this would be a property developer who has land and developments in progress.

However, you can make an election for the trading stock to be transferred at the higher of the original cost or the amount paid by the company.

Starting a new business
If you start a new business as a limited company, you do not have the same problems on transferring a business. However, you do not have the same flexibility available to sole traders or partnerships. Additional costs and compliance requirements attach to limited companies. These include such things as stricter book-keeping requirements, annual filing fees (and penalties for late delivery) with Companies House, possible audit requirements, stricter responsibilities for directors, stricter recording requirements for things such as meetings of directors and shareholders, declaring dividends, issuing shares, etc.

Weighing the benefits
The main taxation reason for trading as a limited company is that the corporation tax rate is:

- 10% on profits up to £10,000 per year,

- Between 10% and 20% on profits between £10,000 and £50,000 per year,

- 20% on profits between £50,000 and £300,000 per year,

- Between 20% and 30% on profits between £300,000 and £1,500,000 per year.

- 30% on profits over £1,500,000 per year.

This may seem a very favourable comparison to the higher income tax rate of 40% for all chargeable income in excess of £28,400 per year.

However, the corporation tax rate applies to profits of the company. The snag here is that the profits must remain in the company to bear the lower corporation tax rates. This is a good strategy if a large amount of the profits need to be ploughed back into the company. If, however, you want to benefit from the profits of the business personally, you have to draw the money out of the business. You can do this either by drawing a salary as a director, or by paying a dividend from the company on your shares. Either way, you will suffer tax at the higher income tax rates on the money you draw.

Drawing a salary

As a director drawing a salary, you will be liable for income tax and class 1 National Insurance contributions. These would be greater in total than the combined tax and class 2 and 4 National Insurance liabilities, for profits up to about £48,000 per year at present rates. In addition, the class 1 National Insurance contributions start to build up an earnings-related supplement to the National Insurance pension when you retire. However, the class 1 liability falls on the company as well as the employee. The liability could be as much as 10% on the employee and 10% on the employer. Class 2 and class 4 contributions give you no extra benefits, but cost less.

HOW?

To draw a salary as a director, you are on the same footing as any other employee. Therefore, if you have not yet done so, you will need to contact your local tax office and register as an employer. They will then send you a pack of documentation to operate a PAYE system. This is the system by which the employer deducts tax and National Insurance from employees and then pays it over to the Inland Revenue once a month. You will then have to work out the deductions on the pay you are drawing as a director, and only draw the net amount.

Warning: There are some different rules for making deductions for directors as opposed to ordinary employees, especially for National Insurance deductions.

Paying a dividend

Paying a dividend does of course mean that you avoid paying the class 1 National Insurance charge on both the company and the employee. The dividend carries a 10% tax credit, and there would be no further tax liability for lower-rate and basic-rate taxpayers. However, higher-rate taxpayers have to pay the additional rate, and if you are not liable to tax, the tax credit is not repayable.

HOW?

To draw a dividend, you pay from the company to yourself the amount you wish to draw, but you must also account to the Inland Revenue for the tax credit. The company must also issue a dividend voucher showing the net dividend paid and the tax credit. Do not forget to declare the dividend on your self assessment tax return.

Often, people running a business as a limited company draw a mixture of salary and dividend.

Providing for a pension

A further advantage of running a business as a limited company is that the company can set up a company pension scheme for its directors (and other employees if required). The contribution limits are far more generous than for self-employed people, and the contributions of the company are tax-deductible from its profits. If you are seriously considering the provision of a pension, a limited company could be a substantial advantage in planning your retirement.

HOW?

The company has to arrange a pension scheme, usually under the auspices of an insurance company which operates such schemes. Details such as who is allowed to join the scheme, what contributions are payable, what benefits are available and when, *etc* are included in the scheme rules. The scheme may be contributory, in which case the employees make some contribution which is matched by the employer, or non-contributory, in which case the employer only makes the contribution, and it is considered as a sort of benefit.

GOING INTO PARTNERSHIP

A partnership is legally defined as a body of persons carrying on business together with a view to profit. One of the most common types of partnership is between a husband and wife. The benefits for tax are such that this is an extremely popular way to carry on business. It confers flexibility of profit-sharing arrangements, which is one of the key advantages.

However, you must bear in mind that being in partnership creates certain **duties and responsibilities**. Also, the relationship between partners needs to be transparently open, because your partner can do things which will affect you – perhaps adversely. Husband and wife partnerships are not often bound by a formal partnership agreement, but if you are entering on a partnership with somebody who is not your spouse, it is extremely wise to draw up a partnership agreement.

If the Inland Revenue are doubtful about the validity of a partnership, they will apply tests to satisfy themselves. These tests include such things as:

● Is there a written partnership agreement?

● Is there any other evidence of a business partnership?

● What is the description of the business on the firm's stationery?

● Who has the authority to operate the business's bank account?

● Whose names appear on the VAT registration?

The presence of these tests indicates that there are tax advantages, and the Inland Revenue want to make sure that they are only taken advantage of by *bona fide* partnerships.

As indicated, one of the main benefits is that the profit from the partnership can be divided out between the partners in a flexible way. Thus, partners who have more allowances and reliefs for tax purposes could have more profit allocated to them in order to use their allowances, reliefs and lower-rate tax band more effectively. This all presumes that the method of sharing the profit is agreeable to all the partners.

This is why husband and wife partnerships are popular. In most cases, the income from the business of a husband and wife partnership goes into the household 'purse'. How it is allocated between husband and wife does not matter except for tax purposes. A further allowance which produces savings is the class 4 National Insurance threshold.

Example

Mr Jones is in business and he employs his wife at a salary of £4,000 a year. His profit after paying his wife's salary is £35,000 for 2000/2001. The tax liability is as follows:

		Husband	*Wife*
Profit		35,000	
Salary			4,000
Personal allowance		4,385	4,385
Taxable		30,615	NIL
Tax due	10% on 1,520	152.00	
	22% on 26,880	5,913.60	
	40% on 2,215	886.00	
		6,951.00	
Class 4 National Insurance – maximum		1,640.45	
Total tax and class 4 liability		£8,592.05	

Now, if Mr Jones took his wife into partnership, their profit figure would be £39,000. If the profits were divided equally, the position would be:

		Husband	Wife
Profit		19,500	19,500
Personal allowance		4,385	4,385
Taxable		15,115	15,115
Tax due	10% on 1,520	152.00	152.00
	22% on 13,595	2,990.90	2,990.90
		3,142.90	3,142.90

Class 4 National Insurance
         Profit   19,500
         Deduct   4,385

		Husband	Wife
	15,115 at 7%	1,058.05	1,058.05
		£4,200.95	£4,200.95

The total tax and Class 4 bill is £8,401.90, compared to £ 8,592.05 if Mr Jones employed his wife, a saving of £190.15.

Question and answer
If it is so beneficial to take somebody into partnership, what is to stop me taking many more relatives, and other people, into partnership?

There is nothing at all to stop you doing this. Many people running a family business bring their children into the partnership when the time is right. However, you must be sure you can work as equals with the people you take into partnership. Also, a partnership creates legal rights and obligations between the partners. One of the most important of these is the concept of joint and several liability. This means that if your partner owes any money, his creditors may pursue other members of the partnership for payment.

Dividing the profit
However, the profit does not have to be divided equally. If, instead of dividing the profit equally, the husband took £32,785 and the wife took £6,215, the result would be as follows:

		Husband	*Wife*
Profit		32,785	6,215
Personal allowance		4,385	4,385
Taxable		28,400	1,830
Tax due	10% on 1,520	152.00	152.00
	22% on 26,880	5,913.60	
	22% on 310		68.20
		6,065.60	220.20
Class 4 National insurance maximum		1,640.45	
Class 4 National insurance			
Profit share	6215		
deduct	4385		
	1830 at 7%		128.10
		£7,706.05	£348.30

The total bill is now £8,054.35, a further saving of £347.55 compared with an equal sharing of the profit.

The key to deciding how to divide profits is to use the allowances and lower-rate tax bands as far as possible. In some cases, as in the above example, it means trading off a smaller charge against a larger one.

HOW?

The division of profits should be shown on the face of your partnership accounts. If each partner has a separate capital account, their share of the profit should be added to their capital account. This division of profits should be the same as that on the partnership self-assessment tax return, boxes 3 to 23 on pages 6 and 7 of the partnership tax return (see Figures 7 and 8).

Question and answer
Can the Inspector of Taxes challenge the division of profits if it seems too artificial?

No. As long as there is nothing in a partnership agreement which forbids it, and as long as the figures in the partnership accounts agree with the tax figures, you may allocate the profits in whatever way you wish.

DISCLAIMING CAPITAL ALLOWANCES

When you are in business you are allowed to claim capital allowances against your profit. These allowances are tax allowances against your profit for the use of equipment, vehicles, *etc.* They are broadly similar to providing for depreciation on these assets used for your business. However, at certain times, the government announces higher rates of capital allowances than the normal 25%. For instance, from July 1997 to June 1998, the rate of allowance for the first year of claiming for an asset was 50%, and since July 1998 it is 40%. The March 2000 budget introduced a 100% rate for investment in computers and e-commerce.

The allowance works by claiming the allowance for the first year, then deducting the amount claimed, then the reduced amount is the basis for the next year's claim. This means that the claims can never exceed the cost of the asset. If the asset is sold, there is a balancing charge or balancing allowance depending on the sale proceeds.

Example

Cost of asset	5,000
First year allowance 50%	2,500
Written down value year 1	2,500
Allowance year 2 at 25% of 2,500	625
Written down value year 2	1,875
Allowance year 3 at 25% of 1875	469
Written down value year 3	1,406
Sold for £1,300	1,300
Balancing allowance year 4	106

Thus, the cost of the asset was £5,000, and it was sold in year 4 for £1,300. It has therefore had a net cost of £3,700. The capital allowances have been:

Year 1	2,500
Year 2	625
Year 3	469
Year 4	106
Total allowances	3,700

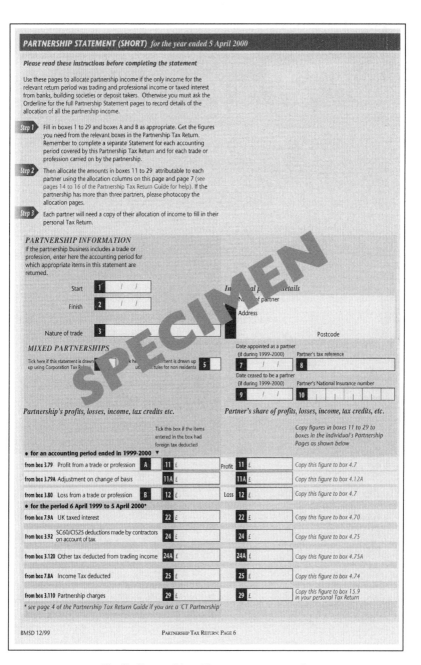

PARTNERSHIP STATEMENT (SHORT) *for the year ended 5 April 2000*

Please read these instructions before completing the statement

Use these pages to allocate partnership income if the only income for the relevant return period was trading and professional income or taxed interest from banks, building societies or deposit takers. Otherwise you must ask the Orderline for the full Partnership Statement pages to record details of the allocation of all the partnership income.

Step 1 Fill in boxes 1 to 29 and boxes A and B as appropriate. Get the figures you need from the relevant boxes in the Partnership Tax Return. Remember to complete a separate Statement for each accounting period covered by this Partnership Tax Return and for each trade or profession carried on by the partnership.

Step 2 Then allocate the amounts in boxes 11 to 29 attributable to each partner using the allocation columns on this page and page 7 (see pages 14 to 16 of the Partnership Tax Return Guide for help). If the partnership has more than three partners, please photocopy the allocation pages.

Step 3 Each partner will need a copy of their allocation of income to fill in their personal Tax Return.

PARTNERSHIP INFORMATION
If the partnership business includes a trade or profession, enter here the accounting period for which appropriate items in this statement are returned.

Start **1** / /

Finish **2** / /

Nature of trade **3**

Individual partner details

Name of partner

Address

Postcode

MIXED PARTNERSHIPS

Tick here if this statement is drawn up ... ment is drawn up using Corporation Tax Rules ... us ... rules for non residents **5**

Date appointed as a partner
(if during 1999-2000) **7** / /   Partner's tax reference **8**

Date ceased to be a partner
(if during 1999-2000) **9** / /   Partner's National Insurance number **10**

Partnership's profits, losses, income, tax credits etc.

Partner's share of profits, losses, income, tax credits, etc.

	Tick this box if the items entered in the box had foreign tax deducted				Copy figures in boxes 11 to 29 to boxes in the individual's Partnership Pages as shown below
• for an accounting period ended in 1999-2000 ▼					
from box 3.79 Profit from a trade or profession **A**	**11** £	Profit **11** £			Copy this figure to box 4.7
from box 3.79A Adjustment on change of basis	**11A** £	**11A** £			Copy this figure to box 4.12A
from box 3.80 Loss from a trade or profession **B**	**12** £	Loss **12** £			Copy this figure to box 4.7
• for the period 6 April 1999 to 5 April 2000*					
from box 7.9A UK taxed interest	**22** £	**22** £			Copy this figure to box 4.70
from box 3.92 SC60/CIS25 deductions made by contractors on account of tax	**24** £	**24** £			Copy this figure to box 4.75
from box 3.120 Other tax deducted from trading income	**24A** £	**24A** £			Copy this figure to box 4.75A
from box 7.8A Income Tax deducted	**25** £	**25** £			Copy this figure to box 4.74
from box 3.110 Partnership charges	**29** £	**29** £			Copy this figure to box 15.9 in your personal Tax Return

* see page 4 of the Partnership Tax Return Guide if you are a 'CT Partnership'

BMSD 12/99   PARTNERSHIP TAX RETURN: PAGE 6

Fig. 7. Partnership self assessment – page 6.

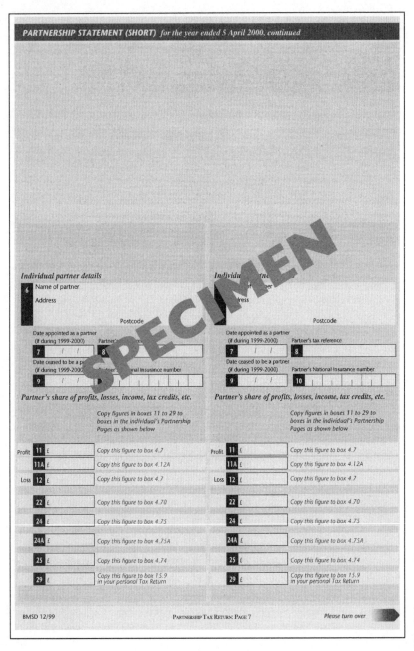

Fig. 8. Partnership self assessment – page 7.

Disclaiming Capital Allowances

Tax tip
Capital allowances do not have to be claimed in their entirety. You have the right not to claim the allowances, or to restrict the claim. This could be advantageous if your income is already not enough to make you taxable even before the allowances.

Example
You have business profits of £6,500. You can claim allowances on assets with a value of £12,000.

	If you claimed full allowances	*If you restricted your claim*
Profits	6,500	6,500
Capital allowances	3,000	2,115
Net amount	3,500	4,385
Personal allowance	4,385	4,385
Taxable	NIL	0
Tax due	NIL	NIL
Capital expenditure carried forward	9,000	10,895

Thus, although there is no difference in the nil tax liability, you have more to carry forward and claim for capital allowances in future years.

HOW?
Work out the restricted amount of allowances you wish to claim, then enter the amounts in box 1.35 of the employment pages (see Figure 3), or boxes 3.61 to 3.70 of the self-employment pages (see Figure 4) of your self-assessment tax return.

USING OVERLAP RELIEF

At the same time as self assessment was introduced, the basis of assessment for self employed people (Schedule D) changed. Previously, it was the 'preceding year basis' (i.e. the profits of the accounting year ending in one tax year were taxed in the next tax year). The new basis, currently in use, is the 'current year basis'. This means that the profits of the accounting year ending in a tax year are taxed in that same year.

There are special rules for calculating the opening years' assessments for a new business, and the closing years when a business finishes. The overall effect is that the exact amount of profits made in the life of a business is assessed to tax. (Under the old system, it was possible for the amount assessed to tax to be different from the amount of profits in the life of the business). This works by way of **overlap relief**.

Overlap relief is a means of giving relief where part of the profits of a business are assessed to tax twice. This can happen in two ways:

1. The calculations for the assessment of profits in the opening years of a new business can mean that part of the profits are taxed twice. This depends on the timing of the start of the new business, and the accounting date used. (In general, if 31st March or 5th April are used as the accounting date, there will not be any 'double taxing').

2. Businesses which were in existence before the change to the 'current year basis' and continued afterwards had special rules for assessing the profits in the 3 year transition period. This could also give rise to some profits being assessed twice, and overlap relief can be claimed.

HOW?
Claim the overlap relief by entering the amounts in box 3.75 (for self employed people on their own) or box 4.9 (for self employed people in partnership).

This overlap relief is not given straight away, but it is carried forward. It can only be used

●   When the business ceases, or

●   When there is a change of accounting date.

HOW?

Enter the amount used in box 3.76 (for self employed people on their own) or box 4.10 (for self employed people in partnership). In any year, if you do not claim the overlap relief, it is carried forward, and you should enter the overlap relief carried forward in box 3.77 (for self employed people on their own) or box 4.11 (for self employed people in partnership).

Tax tip

Do not forget to enter the amount brought forward from the previous year's tax return, then carry it forward to the next one. This way, you will not lose sight of the relief and forget to claim it.

If the overlap can only be used in these two circumstances, think carefully about the ways in which you could use it.

The cessation of business rules can happen

● When the business finishes for good, or

● When the business changes format (for example a sole trader takes on a partner, or vice versa, or when a sole trader or partnership decides to become a limited company).

Obviously, it is not good strategy to cease business permanently just to make use of the overlap relief. But if you are thinking of changing the format, it could be advantageous to think about the timing, particularly if there is a year when profits are high and you may be taxed at the higher rate. Thus, it may be possible to get the relief at 40%, although the original profits taxed twice were only taxed at the standard rate or even the lower rate.

The other circumstance in which you can use the overlap relief is a change of accounting date. This is something over which you have full control. Therefore, it may well be worthwhile to change your accounting date

● If you have high profits which will put you into the higher rate of tax, and

● There is sufficient overlap relief brought forward.

CASE STUDIES

Stephanie starts business as a sole trader

Stephanie is in her mid-20s, and has always dreamed of working for herself. She starts up a small flower shop. She decides to trade on her own, and not as a limited company. Having spoken to other people in business, she decides that this is the least complicated way. If her business takes off, she can then think about making it into a limited company, or taking others into partnership.

Roger starts a limited company

Roger's manufacturing business has expanded rapidly. There are many factors which affect his decision to make the business into a limited company. He has heard horror stories of massive insurance claims for personal damages against others manufacturing similar products. Although he has adequate liability insurance, he still feels nervous, and would like the protection of limited liability. He also has plans for expanding his factory production capacity, and selling into export markets. His generally ambitious plans also include starting a company pension scheme to secure his future. He has two daughters just finishing university courses, who would like to come into the business at some point. He feels that a limited company is the best way to be able to pass on the business to his daughters when he is ready to retire.

PERSONAL TAX EFFICIENCY AUDIT

1. Have you decided on your business format by a conscious decision, or by default?

2. Have you set out the benefits and disadvantages to you of going limited?

3. Are you employing any members of your family in your business? If so, could you take them into partnership?

6

Paying Less Business Tax – 2

Taxes are what we pay for civilised society.
Oliver Wendell Holmes

Even the best run businesses can sometimes make a loss due to circumstances beyond their control. The one compensation is that losses can be used to reduce tax.

USING LOSSES
There are seven main ways in which trading losses can be used:

- By setting them off against other income of the same year, or of the preceding year. You can claim a trading loss as a reduction of your income in either of these years.

- By carrying them forward against future profits of the same trade.

- By carrying back losses in the first four years of assessment of a new trade. The losses may be carried back and offset against any income of the three preceding years.

- By carrying back losses incurred in the twelve months leading up to a permanent discontinuance of a trade. These losses are allowed against profits from the same trade in the three preceding years.

- By setting off trading losses against capital gains in the same year.

- By carrying forward losses from a business which is transferred to a limited company to offset against future income derived from that company, including salary and dividends.

- By claiming post-cessation expenses as a loss in the year in which they are incurred. There may be expenses incurred after a business has ceased, relating to that business, and these can be claimed as a loss in the same year. This is only available up to seven years from the cessation of business.

Deciding which relief to claim

If you make a business loss, you should decide which is the best way to claim it, to gain the best tax advantage.

First, of course, you must work out which reliefs are available – there may be more than one option. So ask yourself if the loss was made in the early years of a business, or the closing year, or after cessation.

Next, work out which tax years would be available for claiming the loss. It could be up to three years back, or indefinitely carried forward.

Then work out what your top rate of tax was in each of those years, and how much of your income was taxed at that top rate. In the case of carrying losses forward, you may have to make an estimate of what profits you expect to be making in the next tax years.

Then make the appropriate claim.

Tax tips
- There are **time limits** for making loss claims. Make sure you make the claim within the time limit. Generally, the time limit is twelve months after 31 January following the end of the year of assessment.

- Remember that if you make a claim to relate the losses back to previous tax years, **extra interest** could well be added on to any repayment of tax. This could tip the balance in favour of making a claim to throw losses back.

- Remember that **capital allowances** can be used to increase a loss, or indeed to create a loss. Also, capital allowances do not have to be claimed in full. If a loss cannot be used fully, you could reduce or disclaim capital allowances.

HOW?
Make a claim for loss relief on your self assessment tax return – in boxes 3.80 to 3.86 on page 3 of the self-employment pages (see Figure 4), or boxes 4.14 to 4.20 on page 1 of the partnership pages if you are in a partnership (see Figure 9).

Question and answer
Is it worth deliberately manufacturing a loss to get the tax relief?

Making a loss is not really something you can or should do 'at will'. You can only make use of a loss when it has genuinely occurred in your business. The advice about this is similar to the advice about expenses.

You are worse off when you make a loss, even after the tax relief. However, one thing you can do is to create or increase a loss by claiming capital allowances.

AVOIDING VAT PITFALLS

VAT – a quick guide

Value Added Tax was conceived as a simple tax. A flat rate of tax was to be added on to all 'outputs' of businesses, and paid over to the Commissioners of Customs and Excise. Part of its complexity today is due to the fact that it is administered by the Customs and Excise rather than by the Inland Revenue. Getting it wrong can be very costly – there are swingeing penalties.

The principle of VAT is that a business adds output tax to its sales. If it sells to another VAT-registered business, that business may claim relief for tax it has paid on its purchases and expenses (its 'input tax') against its own output tax.

Another part of the complexity arises from the way in which VAT is added to outputs of a supplier, then claimed back by the purchaser. The chain goes right along the line from the initial supplier of raw materials to the final consumer, who is not able to claim back the tax. There are also different rates of tax for different items, and a distinction between zero-rated items and exempt items.

The main danger areas in VAT are:

● registration and deregistration

● claiming input tax

● paying output tax.

REGISTERING

Knowing when to register for VAT

A business has to register for VAT if its turnover is above a certain limit. This limit changes from year to year, and at the time of writing it is £52,000 per year. The limit counts for any twelve consecutive months.

Therefore, if you start in business, you should keep a record of your business turnover, month by month. When you reach twelve months, you need only keep a record for these purposes of the last twelve months' figures.

Income for the year ended 5 April 2000

Inland Revenue

PARTNERSHIP (SHORT)

If you have answered 'Yes' to Question 4, fill in Pages P1 and P2. If you want help, look up the box number in the Notes on Partnership at the back of your Tax Return Guide. They are colour-coded to match the form.

You can use these Short Pages if your only partnership income for the year was trading income or taxed interest from banks, building societies and deposit takers (you will see that box numbers do not run consecutively throughout - missing numbers are in the full version of the Partnership Pages). Otherwise you will need the Full Pages, available from the Orderline. You will need to fill in a copy of the appropriate Partnership Pages for each partnership of which you were a member, and for each business carried on by the partnership.

Partnership details

Partnership reference number

4.1

Partnership trade or profession

4.2

- Date you started being a partner (if during 1999-2000) **4.3** / /

- Date you stopped being a partner (if during 1999-2000) **4.4** / /

Your share of the partnership's trading or professional income

Basis period begins **4.5** / / and ends **4.6** / /

- Your share of the profit or loss of this year's account for tax purposes **4.7** £
- Adjustment to arrive at profit or loss for this basis period **4.8** £
- Overlap profit brought forward **4.9** £ ...du... ...o re...sed this year **4.10** £
- Overlap profit carried forward **4.11** £
- Adjustment for farmers' averaging (see Notes, ...PN3 if the ...nership made a loss in 1999-2000) or foreign tax deducted, if tax credit rel... ...not ...ned **4.12** £
- Adjustment on change of bas... **4.12A** £

Net profit for 1999-200... ...oss...ter ...ox 4.13 and enter the loss in box 4.14) **4.13** £

Allowable loss... ...1999-200... **4.14** £

- Loss offset against... ...income for 1999-2000 **4.15** £
- Loss to carry back **4.16** £
- Loss to carry forward (that is, allowable loss not claimed in any other way) **4.17** £
- Losses brought forward from last year **4.18** £
- Losses brought forward from last year used this year **4.19** £

Taxable profit after losses brought forward box 4.13 *minus* box 4.19 **4.20** £

- Add amounts **not** included in the partnership accounts that are needed to calculate your taxable profit (for example, Enterprise Allowance (Business Start-up Allowance) received in 1999-2000) **4.21** £

Total taxable profits from this business box 4.20 + box 4.21 **4.22** £

Class 4 National Insurance Contributions

- Tick this box if exception or deferment applies **4.23**
- Adjustments to profit chargeable to Class 4 National Insurance Contributions **4.24** £

Class 4 National Insurance Contributions due **4.25** £

Fig. 9. Partnership pages of tax return – page 1.

Example

	Turnover	Cumulative turnover 12 months
Month 1	1,000	1,000
Month 2	2,000	3,000
Month 3	4,000	7,000
Month 4	5,000	12,000
Month 5	6,000	18,000
Month 6	6,000	24,000
Month 7	6,000	30,000
Month 8	6,000	36,000
Month 9	6,000	42,000
Month 10	3,000	45,000
Month 11	4,000	49,000
Month 12	2,500	51,500
Month 13	2,000	52,500

You will see that the registration point of £52,000 for any twelve consecutive months has not been reached until the thirteenth month. In keeping a running total, once you get past twelve months, the latest month's figure is added, but the earliest one is then dropped off the total. Once the registration point has been reached, you have 30 days to notify the Customs and Excise of your liability to register. They will then register you from the following month.

You are also liable to register if there are reasonable grounds for believing that your turnover will exceed the registration limit in the next thirty days.

Registering voluntarily

Tax tip
You have the option to register for VAT voluntarily even if your turnover does not reach the registration limit. Why would you want to do this?

The most obvious circumstance in which it might be beneficial to register voluntarily is that you have zero-rated outputs. If you have zero-rated outputs, you do not have to add VAT to your sales. However, because you are registered, you may claim back the input tax on the expenses you incur. This could represent a considerable saving.

If your turnover consists of rated goods or services, it is obvious that having to add VAT to your sales will increase the prices you have to charge your customers. This could make you less competitive, and destroy any advantage of being able to claim back the input tax.

However, it all depends on whether your customers are mainly the general public or other registered traders.

If your customers are mainly the general public, then having to add VAT to your sales is a disadvantage. However, if your customers are mainly other registered businesses, then it does not matter whether you add VAT to your sales or not. If you do add it, your customers can claim it back as their input tax.

HOW?

You register by writing to your local Customs and Excise office (you can find their address in the telephone directory). They will send you a registration form (see Figure 10) to complete. You then have to comply with all the book-keeping requirements, and you will have to complete a VAT return regularly.

Knowing when to deregister

You may have been registered for VAT, but would be better off if you did not have to be registered and add VAT to your sales. If the volume of your business has decreased, you can deregister from VAT. The turnover must be at or below the deregistration limit, which at the time of writing, is £50,000 in any consecutive twelve-month period.

Tax tip
If your business turnover is only marginally over the deregistration limit, you could actually be better off by decreasing your business turnover, so that you can deregister. The saving on VAT could then more than offset the loss in turnover. However, you do need to be sure that there is no prospect of your turnover increasing substantially, at least in the near future.

If you deregister, however, you must pay over VAT on business assets which you had at the date of deregistration, and on which you had originally claimed VAT input tax. The value on which to work out the VAT for these purposes is the value of identical or similar goods of the same age and condition. However, if the VAT on these business assets does not exceed £250, you may ignore it for these purposes.

HOW?

You deregister from VAT by writing to your Customs and Excise office to tell them that you wish to deregister. You will be sent a Final VAT return to complete up to the date of deregistration.

Value Added Tax

Application for Registration

Before you start, please read the Notice "Should I be registered for VAT?". The notes in part 2 will help you to answer the questions on this form. If you do not answer the questions correctly it may take longer to register you and give you a registration number. Write clearly in black ink and use CAPITAL LETTERS.

1   Please give your full name
- *if you are a limited company give your company name*
- *if you are a partnership give your trading name. If you do not have a trading name give the names of all the partners*

Name:

2   Please give your trading name (if different from the name given at 1)

Trading name:

3   Please give the address of your principal place of business
- *this should be where the day-to-day running of your business takes place*

Business address:

Post code:

Phone no:

Fax no:

4   Describe your main business activity

5   Who owns the business?
- *If you are a partnership please remember to fill in form VAT 2 as well as this form*

Please tick ☑

Limited company ☐   Give details from your certificate of incorporation:

Certificate number   Date of certificate

Sole proprietor ☐   Partnership ☐

Other ☐   If other, give details below:

6   (a) Has your business been transferred to you as a going concern?
- *only give details here if you are taking over an existing business from someone else or if you have changed the legal status of your business*

Please tick ☑

Yes ☐ Give details below: No ☐ Go to 7

Date of transfer

Name of previous owner

VAT registration number of previous owner

SPECIMEN

Fig. 10. VAT registration form.

6 (b) Do you want to keep the previous owner's VAT number?

- to keep the number you and the previous owner will have to fill in a form VAT 68 as well

Please tick ✓   Yes ☐   No ☐

7 Please give your bank details

- this question must be completed in all cases

Bank sort code   Account number

or Girobank account number

Please tick box if you do not have a bank account ☐

8 Do you use a computer for accounting?

- if you use a computer let us know the type of computer and software you use, in a separate letter

Please tick ✓   Yes ☐   No ☐

9 Have you made any taxable supplies yet?

- if you are not sure what 'taxable supply' means paragraph 2 in part 1 of the Notice will help you
- if you have not yet made any taxable supplies you **must enclose evidence** to show that you are going to in the future

Please tick ✓

Yes ☐ I made my first supply on
No ☐ but I intend to start on

10 Have your taxable supplies in the past 12 months or less gone over the registration limit?

Please tick ✓

Yes ☐ I went over the limit on
No ☐

11 Do you expect the taxable supplies you will make in the next 30 days alone will go over the registration limit?

Please tick ✓

Yes ☐ Go to 12
No ☐ Go to 13

12 From what date must you be registered for VAT?

- if you have answered Yes to either question 10 or 11 then give the date from which you **have** to be registered (note 12 in part 2 of the Notice will help you)
- if you want to be registered from an earlier date fill in the date in the box provided

I have to be registered from
I would like to be registered from this earlier date

13 I do not need to be registered but I want to be registered

- only answer this question if you have not yet reached the registration limit but want to be registered on a voluntary basis

I want to be registered from

14 Please give the value of taxable supplies you think you will make in the next 12 months

- remember to include zero-rated supplies in this figure

Fig. 10 – continued

15 What value of goods are you likely to sell to or buy from other European Union countries in the next 12 months?

Sell £

Buy £

16 Do you want exemption from registration because all your supplies are zero-rated?

- *if you are asking for exemption from registration enter the expected value of your zero-rated supplies in the next 12 months, in the box provided.*

Please tick ☑

Yes ☐   Value of zero-rated supplies
No ☐   £

17 Do you think you will be repaid VAT regularly?

- *tick Yes if you think the VAT on what you sell will normally be less than the VAT on what you buy*

Please tick ☑

Yes ☐   No ☐

18 Are there any other VAT registrations you are, or have been involved in, in the last 24 months?

- *give the registration numbers of any businesses you have been involved in, in the boxes provided. If you are a partnership or a limited company this means any businesses which any partners or directors have been involved in*

- *Continue on a separate sheet if necessary*

Please tick ☑

Yes ☐   No ☐

Registration numbers of other businesses:

19 Please complete and sign the declaration

Declaration

I,

(enter your full name in CAPITAL LETTERS) declare that the information given on this form and contained in any accompanying document is true and complete.

Signature

Mr, Mrs, Miss, Ms

Date

Please tick ☑

Proprietor ☐   Director ☐
Trustee ☐   Partner ☐
Company Secretary ☐   Authorised official ☐

For office use

Local office code and registration number		E D R	D M Y	Stagger	Status

Name			Trade classification	Taxable Turnover
Trade name				

Rept.	Vol.	Oversize name address	Comp. user	Group Div	Intg.	Overseas	Intg. EC	Value of Sales to EC	Value of Purchases from EC
☐	☐	☐	☐	☐	☐	☐	☐		

Registration	Obligatory/Voluntary	Exemption	Intending	Transfer of Regn No.
Approved - Initial/date				
Refused - Initial/date				
Form issued - Initial/date	VAT9/ other	VAT 8	Letter	Approval letter

VAT 1   Page 2R(11/95)

Fig. 10 – continued

Business splitting

You may think it is possible to get round the need to register for VAT by splitting a business into two or more sections, each of which is below the registration limit. Thus, if a shop has a turnover of £60,000 per year, is it possible to say that there are two businesses, one consisting of tobacco and cigarette sales, the other of confectionery and newspaper sales, each with a turnover below £52,000 per year? The answer is no. The Customs and Excise have anti-avoidance powers to stop this. In consequence, businesses must be genuinely separate to be 'disaggregated'.

This means that, amongst other things, the following characteristics must be there:

● Separate ownership – either the husband must own one business, and the wife the other, or one spouse owns one business, and a partnership or limited company owns the other.

● Separate equipment and premises. Normally, separate businesses must operate from separate premises and use separate equipment.

● Records must be kept separately for each business.

● Invoices to and from each business must be in the name of that business.

● Wages paid to employees must be paid separately by each business.

● For income tax purposes, each business must be separate.

CLAIMING INPUT TAX

The basic principle of claiming input tax is that you may claim for items that can be attributed, either directly or indirectly, to taxable supplies you make.

Zero-rated or exempt – the vital difference

This distinction between **zero-rated** and **exempt** items is crucial. If your output consists of zero-rated items, you are allowed to offset input tax against the output tax on your sales. However, if your output consists of exempt items, you may not deduct the input tax. There are special rules and calculations for a business which has partial exemption, i.e. a mix of rated and exempt items.

Distinguishing business and private items

You may only claim back input tax on business items. This may seem an obvious point, but a surprisingly large number of people try to claim back input tax on private items.

Getting the right documentation

In order to claim input tax, you must have a valid tax invoice from the supplier. To be valid it must:

● have the supplier's VAT number on it

● have the supplier's name and address

● be addressed to you

● be dated

● show the detail of the goods or services supplied

● show the total amount before tax

● show the tax rate

● show the amount of tax

● show the total amount including tax.

However, a 'less detailed tax invoice' is allowed for goods sold if the total amount is less than £100. This less detailed tax invoice need only show:

● the supplier's name and address, and VAT registration number

● the date

● the description of the goods

● the total amount including tax

● the tax rate.

Therefore, VAT input tax is not claimable on delivery notes, or *pro forma* invoices, or if the invoice states 'this is not a tax invoice'.

Specific exclusions

Certain items are specifically excluded for the purpose of claiming input tax. Below are some of the most important.

Motor cars

Input tax cannot be claimed on the cost of a motor car if there is any private use of that motor car. This rule is interpreted very strictly by Customs and Excise. In practice, it is very rare to get a claim for input tax on a motor car allowed. The circumstances have to be such that there is no possibility of private use. Note however the following:

● VAT on lease rentals of cars and contract hire of cars may be claimed, but only up to a maximum of 50%

● VAT on vans, lorries, motor cycles, *etc* can be claimed as long as all the normal conditions are met.

Entertaining
VAT on the cost of entertaining customers cannot be claimed as input tax. This applies whether the customer is from this country or overseas. Entertaining is interpreted widely, and covers almost any type of hospitality.

However, entertaining staff is allowable. If there is an occasion when staff and guests or customers are also present, the cost should be apportioned. Only the input tax attributable to the staff may be claimed.

Directors' accommodation
VAT incurred on supplying any domestic accommodation for a director of a company is not claimable. However, hotel costs for directors (and employees) is claimable. Once again if there is accommodation for a mixture of directors, staff, and guests or customers, the amount must be apportioned, and only the costs for directors and staff may be claimed.

Non-payment
If you do not pay your supplier, for whatever reason, then you may not reclaim the tax. The supplier, if he writes off your debt, will inform the Customs and Excise of your name and address.

PAYING OUTPUT TAX

It is important to charge the correct rate of tax on your supplies. The principle is that you, as a taxable person, must account for VAT at the right rate on taxable supplies you make. Difficulties sometimes arise in deciding what is the correct rate of tax, and what constitutes a taxable supply.

Food products – what is zero-rated?
In deciding what is zero-rated and what is standard-rated, be especially aware of the regulations concerning food.

The general rule is that food products are zero-rated. This includes:

● food for human consumption

● animal feeding stuffs

● seeds or other propagation of plants coming within the above two categories

● live animals generally used as food for human consumption.

However, there are several important exceptions. Perhaps the most obvious is **catering**. Food supplied in the course of catering is standard-rated. But what is catering? It is described as any supply of food or drink for consumption on the premises where it is sold. Also within this category is the sale of takeaway foods, i.e. hot food sold for consumption off the premises.

But where do you draw the line between, say, a takeaway curry, and a loaf of bread that is sold at a bakery while it is still hot? There are detailed guidelines, and you have to work out for yourself what category your sales come under. Obviously, the penalty for getting it wrong could be great.

Other important exceptions which are standard-rated are:

● Confectionery and chocolate products. There is a fairly detailed distinction between zero-rated and standard-rated items. For instance, chocolate-covered biscuits are standard-rated, but chocolate spread is zero-rated. Cakes are zero-rated, but compressed fruit and nut bars are standard-rated. Toffee as a confectionery is standard-rated, but toffee apples are zero-rated. You begin to see how complex these matters can be.

● Ice cream, and similar frozen products.

● Alcoholic drinks.

● Non-alcoholic beverages such as fruit juices, syrups, concentrates, etc. However, tea, coffee, cocoa, and milk are still zero-rated.

● Crisps, salted or roasted nuts.

● Home-brewing materials.

Fuel scale charges

If you claim VAT input tax relief on fuel for cars, and you have any private use during the VAT period, then you must add a 'scale charge' to your VAT output tax which you pay over to Customs and Excise. This represents a taxable supply.

This scale charge is a fixed amount, dependent on the size of the engine of the car, as shown in the table on page 78. However, it is fixed irrespective of the amount of private usage you have of the car. No matter whether you use the car 90% for private use or 5%, the scale charge is the same.

Table of scale charges				
	3 months' charge	VAT due	1 months' charge	VAT due
Diesel engine cars				
up to 2000cc	£232	£34.55	£77	£11.46
over 2000cc	£295	£43.93	£98	£14.59
Petrol engine cars				
up to 1400cc	£256	£38.12	£85	£12.65
1401cc–2000cc	£325	£48.40	£108	£16.08
over 2000cc	£478	£71.19	£159	£23.68

Tax tip

If the total amount spent on fuel for cars is below the amount of the 'charge' figure shown in the table, you are better off not claiming the input tax on the fuel. Otherwise, the scale charge would exceed the input tax you claim.

Supplies of goods for private purposes

If you are registered for VAT, you must pay over output tax on any supplies for which you have recovered input tax, when you take those goods out of the business for private use. If, for example, you own a clothing shop, and take clothes for your own or your family's use, you must account for output tax. The amount at which you must calculate the tax is the cost to the business, not the normal selling price.

Non-business use of assets

If a business asset is made available without charge, for a non-business use, then output tax must be accounted for on the full cost to the business of making the asset available.

Deemed supply on deregistration

Where a business deregisters, there is a 'deemed' supply of the goods and assets held at the time of deregistration. If VAT input tax had previously been claimed, then it must be paid over as output tax (calculated on the value to the business of the goods in their present state at deregistration). However, if the VAT on the deemed supply does not exceed £250, it may be disregarded.

Barter and exchange

If a transaction does not involve a money exchange, it should nevertheless be calculated for the purpose of paying over output tax. This applies to goods or services. Therefore, if there is any barter or exchange of goods or services, the normal commercial values must be taken into account, for input tax and output tax.

BUYING A BUSINESS

It is important to differentiate between:

● buying a business as a **going concern**

● buying the **assets** of a business

● buying the **shares** in a company which is carrying on a business.

There are significant differences in the tax treatment of these three methods. For example, the VAT treatment is quite different.

VAT

If you buy a business as a **going concern**, there is no VAT to pay on the transaction. If you buy **assets** of a business, there is VAT to be charged by the seller. If you buy the **shares** in a company, there is no VAT on the transaction but there is a continuing VAT implication. If you buy the shares of the company, then you are becoming an owner, or part owner of the business. The company's VAT registration is not affected, and you inherit any possible liabilities to VAT which may emerge at a later date. Also, the company may be part of a VAT group of companies, and all members of a VAT group are liable for each other's VAT liabilities. If one member of the group became insolvent, the Customs and Excise could come back on other members of the group to pay the liability of the insolvent member.

Even when buying a business as a going concern, you need to be vigilant. In this transaction, you are asked by the Customs and Excise whether you want to take over the registration of the existing business. If you say yes to this, once again you inherit the existing business's VAT liabilities.

Stamp duty

The stamp duty treatment is also different. If you buy shares in the company, there is stamp duty to pay at 0.5% on the value of the shares. If you buy the business as a going concern, or the assets of the business, stamp duty is payable on a sliding scale between 0% and 2% depending on the value. You therefore need to work out the stamp duty in each case.

Corporation tax and income tax

If you buy the shares in a company, and it continues to carry on the same trade, then any losses which may have accumulated are available to carry forward against future profits. Any assets on which capital allowances have been claimed will simply continue to be carried forward at their written down value.

If you buy the business as a going concern, or the assets of a business, you are treated as starting a new business for income tax purposes. The price which you paid for the assets will be their cost for the purposes of capital allowances. It does not matter what value they had been written down to by the predecessor; you start off at the price you paid.

SELLING A BUSINESS

Selling a business gives rise to the same sort of considerations as buying a business, but from the other side of the fence. However, there are certain additional considerations.

Selling a company

If the business you are selling is a limited company, then you need to consider the way in which you sell it. A buyer may merely want to buy the business as a going concern, or the assets of the business, without buying the shares which give them ownership of the company. However, from your point of view, this presents a difficult problem.

If a company sells assets or the business as a going concern, then the company is liable to capital gains tax on the transaction. Further, when you want to get your money out of the company, there is a further capital gains or corporation tax charge.

By far the best and simplest means of selling a business owned by a company is to sell the shares of the company. This way, there is only one capital gains tax charge.

HOW?
The way in which you sell a limited company will depend largely on your negotiating skills, and the expertise of your solicitor in drawing up the sale document in the right form. Make sure there are no loose ends.

Timing the sale

If you want to sell a business, either in the form of a limited company or otherwise, you should think about the timing very carefully. The most important current relief affected by timing is retirement relief from capital gains tax.

Retirement relief

Retirement relief is available to individuals aged 50 or over (or who are forced to retire earlier through ill health) who sell their business, or part of their business.

Warning

The relief is not available simply on the sale of some assets of the business, if the business itself continues. It must be the sale of the whole or an identifiable part of a business.

The relief is available after you have had the business for one year. At that point, you are eligible for relief on 10% of the gain on the sale. Relief continues to increase on a monthly basis until you get the maximum 100% relief after you have had the business ten years.

There is a maximum relief given under these rules as follows:

● Full relief (at the percentage arrived at as described above) is given up to £150,000 of gains.

● Between £150,000 and £600,000, one half of the relief is given.

● There is no relief on any gain above £600,000.

HOW?

To claim retirement relief, tick column H on page 2 of the capital gains pages with your self assessment tax return, and enter 'Retirement relief claimed' in column O on page 3. Pages 2 and 3 are illustrated in Figure 11.

Phasing out

Retirement relief is being phased out from 6th April 1999. It will be completely abolished from 6th April 2003. This relief will be replaced by tapering relief. The phasing out is being achieved by reducing the ceiling on gains qualifying for relief as follows:

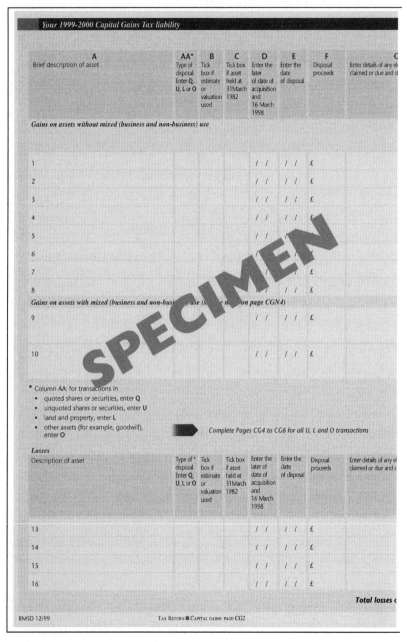

Fig. 11. Capital gains pages of tax return: page 2.

ctions made, reliefs ate amount (£)	H Chargeable Gains after reliefs but before losses and taper	I Enter 'Bus' if business asset	J Taper rate	K Losses deducted			L Gains after losses	M Tapered gains (gains from column L x % in column J)
				K1 Allowable losses of the year	K2 Income losses of 1999-2000 set against gains	K3 Unused losses b/f from earlier years		
	£		%	£	£	£	£	£
	£		%	£	£	£	£	£
	£		%	£	£	£	£	£
	£		%	£	£	£	£	£
	£		%	£	£	£	£	£
	£		%	£	£	£	£	£
	£		%	£	£	£	£	£
	£		%	£			£	£
	£	Bus	%	£	£	£	£	£
	£			£	£	£	£	£
	£		%	£	£	£	£	£
Total	**8.1** £ Total column H			**8.5** £ Total column K2	**8.6** £ Total column K3			**8.3** £ Total column M

ctions made, reliefs ate amount (£)	Losses arising	
		11 Attributed gains from UK resident trusts (enter the name of the Trust on Page CG7) £
		12 Attributed gains from non UK resident trusts (enter the name of the Trust on Page CG7) £
		Total of attributed gains **8.4** £
	£	box 8.3 + box 8.4 **Total taxable gains** £
	£	Copy to box 8.7 on Page CG8 and complete Pages CG4 to CG6 for all U, L and O transactions
	£	
	£	
f year	**8.2** £	

Fig. 11. Capital gains pages of tax return: page 3.

Tax year	100% relief on first	50% relief on next
2000/2001	£150,000	£450,000
2001/2002	£100,000	£300,000
2002/2003	£50,000	£150,000
2003/2004 onwards	£ nil	£ nil

Tapering relief

The new form of relief that replaced both retirement relief and indexation relief from 6 April 1998 is tapering relief. This works by reducing the gain chargeable to capital gains tax by reference to the length of time the asset has been held from 6 April 1998. The taper is more generous for business assets than for personal assets. The maximum time to count for taper relief is ten years for non-business assets, and, since 6 April 2000, four years for business assets. This is done by reducing the gain chargeable to capital gains tax by a certain percentage for each year the asset has been held after 6 April 1998. The maximum taper relief is 75% for businesses after four years and 40% for non-business assets after ten years. The full scale of the tapering is shown in the table below.

Number of whole years asset held	Percentage of gain chargeable Business assets	Non-business assets
Less than 1	100	100
1	87.5	100
2	75	100
3	50	95
4	25	90
5	—	85
6	—	80
7	—	75
8	—	70
9	—	65
10 or more	—	60

Timing the sale

The timing of the sale of the business could therefore be crucial in saving tax. In the early years from 1998/99, there should be much more benefit in retirement relief, although this will gradually reduce. However, the 100% relief will ultimately be replaced by a relief which does not reach 100%. There will reach a point towards the end of the phasing out of retirement relief when the relief of one or other of the methods could be beneficial.

Therefore, if there is the possibility of a sale towards the end of the phase-out period, and particularly if it comes around the end of the tax year, you will need to consider very carefully whether to make the sale before or after the end of the tax year.

USING ELECTRONIC FILING

If you use the newly-available facility for filing your VAT returns or your end of year PAYE returns, and pay any tax due electronically, you benefit from a one-off discount of £50, or a double discount of £100 for both PAYE and VAT.

CASE STUDIES

Jane claims losses against capital gains

Jane has sold her business. She is not old enough to claim retirement relief, has not been forced to sell through illness, and does not wish to 'roll over' the gain by buying new business assets. However, she made a loss in the final year of business, and she decides, in consultation with her accountant, that the best way of claiming loss relief is to set the loss against her capital gains.

Fred thinks about registering for VAT

Fred started a new business about 18 months ago. It has shown good growth since then, and he has realised that he does not know whether he should have registered for VAT or not. He does the exercise of adding up his turnover since he started, and dropping off the first month's figure when he reached the thirteenth month. This way he keeps a record of his 'running total', i.e. the turnover for the last twelve months at all times.

Having done this exercise, he realises that he should have registered two months ago. He contacts the Customs and Excise office straight away, to register for VAT. He realises that he will have to face penalties, but prefers to sort it out now rather than leave it to become a bigger problem later on.

Darby and Joan deregister from VAT

Darby and Joan have been running a small hotel for some years, and they are registered for VAT. Of late, however, the turnover has been fairly static, and the VAT registration limit has been creeping up. Due to their age, they would like to take life a little easier, although they are not quite ready to sell up yet. Their turnover is now only £1,000 above the deregistration limit.

They decide therefore to shut the hotel during February, when trade was at its lowest ebb. This will reduce the turnover, and allow them to deregister. They will then not have to do the quarterly chore of the VAT return, and find that even though they have reduced their turnover, they are not much worse off. They have been able to save a little on their overheads, due to being closed for one month, and they do not have to pay over the VAT on their turnover (although this is partly offset by not being able to reclaim VAT on their expenses).

PERSONAL TAX EFFICIENCY AUDIT

1. If you have made a loss, have you thought about how it can be used for tax purposes?

2. If you are not registered for VAT, do you have an adequate system for tracking your turnover? Have you worked out whether it would be advantageous to register voluntarily?

3. If you are registered for VAT, do you know all the 'quirks' of VAT as it applies to your business? Have you taken professional advice about this?

7

Paying Less Capital Gains Tax – 1

The inevitable consequences of being too fond of glory –
Taxes upon every article which enters into the mouth,
or is placed under the foot … Taxes upon everything
on earth, and the waters under the earth.

Rev. Sydney Smith

USING YOUR ANNUAL ALLOWANCE

As with income tax, everybody has a **personal allowance** for capital
gains tax purposes. For the 2000/2001 tax year the allowance is £7,200
per person. There is also a degree of 'allowance' in the way in which
capital gains tax is charged.

Capital gains tax is charged by adding the amount of the gain to your
other investment income charged to income tax, and charging tax at the
top marginal rate for savings. This could result in a charge at two
different rates.

Example
Your income for the 2000/2001 tax year is £25,000, and you have capital
gains of £16,000 for the same year. The tax is worked out as follows:

Income		25,000
Personal allowance		4,385
Taxable		20,615
Income tax due:		
10% on 1,520		152.00
22% on 19,095		4,200.90
Total income tax due		4,352.90
Capital gains	16,000	
Annual exemption	7,200	
Taxable	8,800	

Taxable:

7,785 at 20%	1,557.00
1,015 at 40%	406.00
Total capital gains tax	1,963.00

You will therefore be able to pay less capital gains tax if you can use up your personal allowance, or if you can keep your chargeable tax to the next lowest band. In the above example, if you had been able to reduce your gain chargeable to tax by £1,015, you would have avoided paying tax at the 40% rate.

Tax tip
Remember also that a husband and wife each have a personal allowance and all the reduced-rate tax bands.

Using losses

So how can you keep your capital gains down to the limits to save tax? One important tool is to use the losses which may be available. All transactions producing capital gains or losses within the same tax year are merged together for tax purposes.

Tax tip
If you have gains which are over the threshold limit, consider whether you may be able to do any other transactions which would produce a loss for capital gains purposes.

Example
You have various stocks and shares, and you have actively traded several of them during the tax year. So far, you have produced gains of £7,300. If you can produce losses of £100, you could reduce your gains to the threshold limit and avoid any tax liability.

Tax tip
It may be possible to establish a loss without actually disposing of any assets. If you have assets which have decreased in value, and are now of negligible value, you can make a claim to 'crystallise' the loss. In practice, this applies most frequently to shares in companies which are no longer of any value. For instance, some years ago, the shares in Maxwell Communications became of no value following the death of Robert Maxwell. The Inland Revenue recognises shares as being of negligible value when their value has decreased to 5% or less of their

nominal value. Therefore, if £1 shares are worth 5p or less, they are recognised for this purpose.

The advantage of this provision is that you do not have to declare them as being of negligible value straight away. You may wait until you can benefit from the declaration, and then make the claim for the loss.

HOW?

Losses are set off against gains automatically. No special claim is needed. Enter all your transactions on pages 2 and 3 of the capital gains pages of your self assessment tax return (See Figure 11). The gains are totalled and the losses are totalled separately. The gains are then entered in box 8.7 of page 8 of the capital gains pages. The losses are entered in box 8.10.

Keeping your gains within the limits

Another way of utilising the threshold limit is to ensure that your gains come up to the limit.

Example

You have made gains so far in the tax year of £4,000. If you can make further gains of up to £3,200, you will still not be liable to tax, because you are still within your limit.

Timing

You may think that it is not always straightforward or easy to make gains or losses. The above examples show the sorts of circumstances when it is most appropriate to be able to take advantage of the threshold limits.

The approach of the end of the tax year is often the best time to be able to do these sort of transactions. As you approach 5 April, you have the choice of whether to carry out transactions before or after that date.

Tax tip

Carrying out transactions before 5 April means that they fall into the present tax year, and could be of use in mitigating this year's tax burden.

It could also be of advantage to postpone transactions until after that date. For instance, you may have made relatively modest gains of, say, £2,000, and you want to carry out another transaction which will show a loss of, say, £1,000. If you did it before 5 April, you would reduce a £2,000 gain to a £1,000 gain, and there would be no tax liability in either case. Therefore the loss has been of no practical value to you. If you did it after 5 April, the £1,000 loss would be available for the following year, when it might be of use to you.

Trading assets

The other point which becomes obvious is that you have to be able to have assets which will give you the opportunity to trade at a gain or a loss, more or less at will. The assets which are most easily traded are stocks and shares. If you have a portfolio, you have a variety of stocks and shares, and there may well be some amongst them which meet the right conditions.

USING THE LOWER-RATE BANDS

As we have seen, the rate of capital gains tax depends on the level of income tax that you pay. In effect, all your 'income', whether from income sources or capital gains, is aggregated to arrive at your true tax liability.

Therefore, when considering your capital gains position, you should not look at it in isolation. If you have made a capital gain in a tax year, you should think about your overall tax position. For instance, are there any loss claims you could make? Could you make pension contributions? Are there other allowances or reliefs of which you could take advantage? These will all impact upon the income tax position, and the effect 'follows through' to the capital gains tax position.

BED AND BREAKFASTING

A method by which you used to be able to take advantage of these provisions was called 'bed and breakfasting'. Unfortunately, it was effectively abolished in the Spring Budget of 1998. It involved selling an asset – usually stocks or shares – and buying it back the next day. The sale established either a gain or a loss which was used for the purposes mentioned above. The repurchase the next day meant that it was then deemed to be acquired at that price for any future capital gains purposes.

Since the Spring Budget of 1998, however, any purchases and sales of identical assets within a 30-day period are matched with each other for capital gains tax purposes. The advantage of doing this was therefore lost.

However, there are some options still left open:

- You could sell the shares, and not buy them back for 30 days. This of course greatly increases the risk factor, since the price may have moved adversely in that time.

- You could sell the shares, and repurchase different shares. However, any purchase of shares should be made first and foremost on investment criteria.

- You could sell the shares, and they could be repurchased by your spouse. This, however, would have to be compatible with your overall tax planning, and indeed your overall marriage arrangements.

CASE STUDIES

Nora postpones selling shares

It is the middle of March, and Nora needs to replace her car. She has a portfolio of shares, and the most obvious way of raising the money is to sell some shares. However, she knows that she will show a gain for capital gains tax purposes, and she had already made some capital gains earlier in the tax year. She pays income tax, and has used up her 22% tax band to the full. If she sells shares now, she will incur a capital gains tax liability at 40% to be paid next January.

She thinks about the problem, and comes up with two possible solutions. She could pay for urgent repairs to her car, and then keep it. However, the cost of these repairs will be quite large, and the car could still not be very reliable. It might then have to be sold, but this would not be until the new tax year, so she would not have the same immediate capital gains tax problem.

The other solution is to get a short-term overdraft from the bank, then sell the shares in the new tax year. The cost of the overdraft interest for such a short period will be nothing like the cost of the capital gains tax. She goes for this option.

Victor and Hyacinth transfer some shares

Victor and Hyacinth are married, and have not previously paid much attention to planning their finances in a tax-efficient way. Now they have been encouraged to do so, approaching the end of the tax year. All the investments are in Victor's name, and he has not traded any in the current tax year. They realise that transferring some of the shares to Hyacinth will enable her to use her personal allowance and some of her lower-rate tax band.

To do this, Victor transfers some shares valued at £30,000 (which make a profit for capital gains tax purposes of just under £6,000) to Hyacinth. He has used up some of his capital gains tax threshold, and she now has income in her own name.

PERSONAL TAX EFFICIENCY AUDIT

1. Do you know how much gain you have made for capital gains tax purposes when you sell shares?

2. Do you have surplus allowances or lower-rate tax bands available?

3. Do you have any assets on which you could establish a loss?

8

Paying Less Capital Gains Tax – 2

> Neither will it be, that a people overlaid with taxes
> should ever become valiant and martial.
>
> Francis Bacon

USING THE RELIEFS

A number of reliefs are available – some to people in specific circumstances – which can reduce or postpone your capital gains tax liability. Some are deferments only, but it is sometimes possible to defer capital gains almost indefinitely. When you die, there is no capital gains tax to pay on whatever passes from your estate to your survivors. Whoever inherits your assets starts off with a 'clean sheet' of the assets at their probate value for capital gains tax purposes.

HOW?
All reliefs are claimed on page 3 of the capital gains pages of your self assessment tax return, (See Figure 11). Claim reliefs in column G, entering the amounts against each individual gain.

ROLL-OVER RELIEF

This is a relief given to people who are carrying on a business – either alone or in partnership. If you sell any business assets, there might be a capital gain liable to tax on the sale. However, if you buy new assets for your business within a certain time limit, the gain may be 'rolled over'. This means that the amount of the chargeable gain on the asset sold is not assessed to capital gains tax, but is used to reduce the cost, for capital gains tax purposes, of the new asset bought. Therefore, if and when the new asset is eventually sold, the gain on the old asset is brought into charge for capital gains tax.

However, the new asset itself may be eligible to roll over the gain if another new asset is bought within the time limit. In this case, the gain from the original asset is rolled over as well as the gain from the one currently being sold. The 'rolling over' process can go on without limitation of the number of times it happens.

Limit on the type of assets

Rollover relief can only be claimed on assets falling within the following categories:

● land and buildings (including permanent or semi-permanent structures in the nature of buildings)

● fixed plant and machinery

● ships, aircraft and hovercraft

● satellites, space stations and spacecraft

● goodwill

● milk quotas, potato quotas and ewe and suckler cow premium quotas.

Example
You bought a factory in April 1991 for £50,000. You used it for your business, then sold it in March 2000 for £110,000. At the same time, you bought a bigger factory for £150,000.

The gain is worked out as follows:

Sale price		110,000
Purchase price	50,000	
Indexation allowance say 30%	15,000	65,000
Gain		£35,000

The rollover relief is given by deducting this chargeable gain of £35,000 from the cost of the new building, i.e.:

Cost of new building	150,000
Less gain rolled over	35,000
	£115,000

The 'base cost' of the new building for capital gains tax purposes is now £115,000.

Question and answer
What if I have received, say, £20,000 for the sale of an asset, but only paid out, say, £15,000 for the replacement asset?

The gain can only be rolled over in full if the amount spent on the new asset is at least equal to the proceeds of sale of the old asset. Otherwise, the amount of the sale proceeds not used to purchase the new asset remains chargeable to capital gains tax.

Example
The same facts as the previous example, except that you bought the new factory for £90,000 only. The chargeable gain is the same – £35,000. The amount of the sale price of the old premises which you have not reinvested is £20,000 (i.e. £110,000 less £90,000).

The amount chargeable to capital gains tax on the sale of the first factory is the lesser of the chargeable gain (£35,000) and the amount not reinvested (£20,000). Therefore, £20,000 is charged to capital gains tax. The cost of the new factory is then reduced by the amount of the gain rolled over, as follows:

Chargeable gain	35,000
Charged to tax	20,000
Amount rolled over	£15,000

The base cost of the new factory then becomes:

Cost of new building	90,000
Less gain rolled over	15,000
New base cost	£75,000

Time limits
The limit within which the new asset can be bought to qualify for the roll-over relief is **between one year before and three years after the sale of the first asset.**
   The normal date for payment of capital gains tax is 31 January following the year of assessment in which the gain was made.

Tax tip
You could have already paid the tax before you purchase a new asset on which the rollover relief can be claimed. In this case, you can make the claim and get a refund of the tax you have paid.

RETIREMENT RELIEF

We looked at retirement relief in some detail in Chapter 6. Retirement relief is also available (until it is completely phased out) on disposals of:

- assets used in an employment or office that you hold

- assets owned by a partner and used in the partnership business

- assets owned by a director or office holder in a company, and used for the business of that company

- assets of a trust, if the assets are shares in a company or assets used in a company business. The beneficiary of the trust must enjoy the benefit of the assets concerned for retirement relief to apply.

The other conditions for retirement relief apply – such as the age at retirement, or ill-health grounds, and the length of holding the assets (with proportionate relief given at 10% from year one, rising to 100% at year ten).

HOLD-OVER RELIEF

Hold-over relief applies to gifts or transfers of business assets or agricultural property 'not at arm's length'. A transaction 'not at arm's length' means one where the transaction is between 'connected persons' and therefore not at a full market value. The definition of 'connected persons' is looked at in Chapter 13 in more detail.

Hold-over relief operates in a similar way to roll-over relief as described above. In other words, the gain is 'held over' until the person acquiring the asset disposes of it. In order to get the relief, both the person making the transfer and the person receiving it must make a joint claim.

This claim can be made for assets used in a business, shares in a trading company, or agricultural property.

The most common scenario for this claim is a person passing on a business to someone in his or her family by gifting the whole business, or assets of the business, to that other person. Although the person receiving the gift has received it free, he or she will have to bear the ultimate capital gains tax liability, unless he or she in turn passes it on to somebody else.

Warning
If the person receiving the gift or transfer becomes non-resident in the UK, then there is a clawback of the held-over gain, and the tax becomes payable.

REINVESTMENT IN SHARES RELIEF

Any chargeable capital gain may be 'rolled over' into the purchase cost of qualifying shares. Qualifying shares are ordinary shares in 'qualifying companies'.

Qualifying companies are those companies:

- not quoted on a recognised stock exchange or the Unlisted Securities Market, and

- which carry out a qualifying trade. A qualifying trade is one which **does not** consist substantially of any of the following:

  - dealing in land, commodities, futures, shares, securities or financial instruments

  - dealing in goods, other than wholesalers or retailers

  - banking, insurance, money-lending, debt factoring, hire-purchase financing, etc

  - leasing or receiving royalties or licence fees

  - legal or accountancy services

  - providing services or facilities for any trade in the above categories.

This relief is very flexible, because it can be limited, if you choose, to any amount up to the full amount of the chargeable gain. This means that you can limit your claim to the right amount needed to reduce your gain to the amount of your annual exemption.

Most stockbrokers have lists of companies which qualify for this relief. If you want to take advantage of it, you should be aware of the increased risk profile due to the fact that the company is not quoted.

Withdrawal of the relief

The relief is withdrawn, and the tax becomes payable, if any of the following happen:

- the shares cease to be 'eligible' shares, i.e. no longer ordinary shares

- the company ceases to be a qualifying company, i.e. by carrying out one of the restricted businesses

- the person holding the shares becomes non-resident in the UK

- any of the shares are involved in a reconstruction, conversion, etc, and exchanged for Corporate Bonds.

CASE STUDIES

Rodney passes on shares to his children

After a bitter boardroom battle, Rodney has gained control of Trotters Trading Company Ltd. Now, approaching retirement age, he wants to start passing some of his shares to his children. He starts making gifts of the shares, year by year, gradually reducing his holdings, and increasing his children's holdings. As the transactions are with connected persons, the proper market value has to be used. However, Rodney and his children claim hold-over relief. They hope that this scenario will repeat itself when his sons and daughters reach retirement age, or capital gains tax is abolished!

Rodney claims roll-over relief

At the same time, the business is expanding, and the company's warehouse is not big enough. The company sells the warehouse, and buys a bigger one. The new one was bought a month before the old one was sold, and is therefore in the right timescale. The company claims roll-over relief on the new warehouse.

Del Trotter claims reinvestment in shares relief

When Del Trotter was ousted from Trotters Trading Company Ltd, the settlement included a handsome payout. He invested this in property, and now has the opportunity to sell the properties at another handsome profit. In order to shelter this from capital gains tax, he reinvests in qualifying shares for reinvestment relief. His mates at the pub have been full of suggestions of companies to invest in. However, he prefers to rely on his stockbroker, and accept their advice of companies to reinvest in. He now has an accountant who has advised him of the optimum amount to reinvest to get the full relief and pay no capital gains tax.

PERSONAL TAX EFFICIENCY AUDIT

1. Are you in business, and seeking to sell an asset? If so, can you plan its replacement to benefit from roll-over relief?

2. Have you planned your retirement? Do the plans include making sure that you qualify for retirement relief, or tapering relief?

3. Do you wish to pass your business on to the next generation of your family? If so, have you considered how to use hold-over relief claims?

4. Are you considering reinvestment in shares relief? If so, have you considered the risk element?

9

Using Exemptions

It was as true as taxes is.
And nothing's truer than them.
Charles Dickens – *David Copperfield*

Several items of income, gains, etc are exempt from various taxes. Remember this – the exemptions have been created by various governments to encourage saving or investment in various forms, or because the income exempted is a special category of some sort.

HOW?

There is no special procedure to claim the exemptions. Just ensure that the income or gain which is exempt is not declared in your self assessment tax return.

UNDERSTANDING EXEMPT INCOME

Some of the items of income exempted from tax are not ones over which you have any control, and they are therefore of no relevance in trying to save tax. Examples of this sort of exemption are:

- additional pensions paid by virtue of gallantry awards

- compensation for mis-sold pensions or bad investment advice

- income from international organisations ✓

- damages and compensation for personal injury.

This list is not exhaustive, but it gives an idea of the sort of things exempted.

However, we will look at some of the most important exempt items over which you do have control.

TESSAs

These Tax Exempt Special Savings Accounts were only available to start up to 5 April 1999. They are fixed five-year term savings accounts with the following restrictions:

● A maximum of £3,000 may be invested in the first year.

● A maximum of £1,800 may be invested in any succeeding year.

● The maximum investment over the five-year term is £9,000.

● There may not be any withdrawal of the capital in the five-year period.

● Interest may be drawn out, but only up to the equivalent of the net amount – i.e. as if tax had been deducted from the interest.

Save-as-you-earn schemes

These are schemes which must have government approval, and are operated by employers in connection with share option schemes. Any interest on these schemes is free of tax, as well as the beneficial treatment of the shares themselves.

HOW?

The only way to benefit from such a scheme is if your employer has it on offer.

National Savings Bank Ordinary Accounts

The first £70 per annum of interest on these accounts is free of tax. These accounts do not pay a great rate of interest, but they are accessible at post offices, and offer instant access to the money.

HOW?

In box 10.8 on page 3 of your self assessment tax return (see Figure 12), make sure you deduct the first £70 of interest before entering the amount.

National Savings Certificates

There are several different forms of certificates. Some have a fixed life of five years, and a fixed rate of interest. Others are linked to the inflation index. They all share the exemption from tax on the interest earned. National Savings Children's Bonus Bonds also have tax-free interest.

Personal Equity Plans

These were only available until 5 April 1999.

All income held in a PEP is free of income tax, and any gains made on selling the assets held in a PEP are free of capital gains tax.

Individual Savings Accounts

From 6 April 1999, the previous tax-exempt investments in TESSAs and PEPs were replaced by ISAs (Individual Savings Accounts). Existing TESSAs and PEPs may continue alongside any new investment in ISAs.

The main features of ISAs are:

● There is a maximum investment of £7,000 per tax year up to 5 April 2001.

● There is an overall investment limit of £50,000.

● Of each year's investment, up to £3,000 (up to 5 April 2001) may be in bank or   building society accounts, and up to £1,000 may be in life assurance policies.

● There is no lock-in period, as there was with TESSAs.

● An ISA may include any combination of bank or building society accounts, stocks, shares, unit trusts, life assurances, or National Savings products.

● All income and capital gains from ISAs are free of all taxes.

Question and answer
Am I limited to choosing any one of the various tax-exempt types of savings?

No. You may take advantage of as many of them as you wish.

Lump sums under personal pensions or retirement annuities

When you take benefits from these policies, you may take a certain amount of the pension fund as a lump sum. The rest must be taken as an annuity for the rest of your life (or the joint lives of you and your spouse). That annuity is taxable. The lump sum is tax free, and there are no restrictions as to what you can do with it. It therefore makes sense to take the maximum lump sum available.

INCOME *for the year ended 5 April 2000*

Q 10 Did you receive any income from UK savings and investments? | NO | YES

If yes, fill in boxes 10.1 to 10.26 as appropriate. Include only your share from any joint savings and investments.

■ *Interest*

● Interest from UK banks, building societies and deposit takers

Taxable amount

- where **no tax** has been deducted — 10.1 £

	Amount **after tax deducted**	Tax deducted	Gross amount **before tax**
- where **tax has** been deducted	10.2 £	10.3 £	10.4 £

● Interest distributions from UK authorised unit trusts and open-ended investment companies (dividend distributions go below)

Amount after tax deducted	Tax deducted	Gross amount before tax
10.5 £	10.6 £	10.7 £

● National Savings (other than FIRST Option Bonds and the first £70 of interest from a National Savings Ordinary Account)

Taxable amount — 10.8 £

● National Savings FIRST Option Bonds

Amount after tax deducted	...deducted	Gross amount before tax
10.9 £	10.	10.11 £

● Other income from UK savings and investments (except dividends)

Amount after tax...	...deducted	Gross amount before tax
10.12 £	10.13 £	10.14 £

■ *Dividends*

● Dividends and other ...lifyi... distribution... ...UK ...anies

Dividend/distribution	Tax credit	Dividend/distribution plus credit
10.15 £	10.16 £	10.17 £

● Dividend distributions from UK authorised unit trusts and open-ended investment companies

Dividend/distribution	Tax credit	Dividend/distribution plus credit
10.18 £	10.19 £	10.20 £

● Scrip dividends from UK companies

Dividend	Notional tax	Dividend plus notional tax
10.21 £	10.22 £	10.23 £

● Non-qualifying distributions and loans written off

	Notional tax	Taxable amount
10.24 £	10.25 £	10.26 £

SPECIMEN

Fig. 12. Page 3 of self assessment tax return.

Termination of employment
Payments such as compensation for loss of employment, redundancy pay, job release allowances and wages *in lieu* of notice are all free of income tax. Therefore, if you are in danger of losing your job, ensure that your employer pays you in the most tax-efficient way.

Social security benefits
Make sure about the taxable status of your benefits. Some are taxable, some are not. Figure 13 shows which benefits are taxable and which are not. Only declare on the tax return the items which are taxable. Boxes 11.1 to 11.9 on page 4 of your self assessment tax return (see Figure 14) show which items you should declare.

Exempt pensions
Certain pensions are exempt. Make sure that you do not declare these. These include:

● voluntary pensions not arising from past employment or not paid by past employers or their successors

● members of the armed forces receiving disability or wound pensions

● pensions awarded for retirement due to an injury on duty or due to a work-related illness

● pensions payable to non-UK residents under various acts including the Overseas Service Act 1958, the Pensions (India, Pakistan and Burma) Act 1955, the British Nationality Act 1981, etc. These pensions are mainly for overseas service in the ex-colonies

● pensions to war widows for death of their husbands in service in the armed forces, or wartime service in the merchant navy

● German and Austrian pensions for victims of Nazi persecution.

RENT A ROOM
This is a scheme to exempt from tax the first £4,250 of rents you receive from letting out a room in your main residence. The first £4,250 of rents you receive are tax free, and you have to pay tax only on any surplus above £4,250 for the year. The limit of £4,250 is per household, not per person. Therefore, if you share a house, and each person lets out a room, the £4,250 is shared between them. You

Taxable	Not taxable
Incapacity benefit – except for the benefit for the first 28 weeks	Educational maintenance allowance
	Family credit
Industrial death benefit when paid as a pension	Hospital patients' travel expenses
	Housing benefits
Income support – if it is paid subject to availability for work (i.e. unemployed), or if the claimant is on strike	Income support apart from the taxable part
	Social fund payments
	Student grants
	Uniform and clothing grants
Invalid care allowance	Industrial death benefit
Invalidity allowance – when paid with retirement pension Jobseeker's allowance (up to the 'taxable minimum')	Disablement benefit
	Incapacity benefit for the first 28 weeks
	Maternity allowance
Job-release allowance	Sickness benefit
Old person's pension	Attendance allowance
Retirement pension	Back-to-work bonus
Statutory maternity pay	Child benefit
Statutory sick pay	Child dependency additions
Income support – when paid to unemployed and strikers	Child's special allowance
	Pensioners' Christmas bonus
Unemployment benefit	Disability living allowance
Widowed mother's allowance	Disability working allowance
Widow's pension	Employment rehabilitation allowance
	Fares to school
	Guardian's allowance
	Home improvement, repair and insulation grants
	Invalidity allowance – when paid with invalidity pension
	Invalidity pension
	Jobfinder's grant
	Jobmatch payments
	Jobseeker's allowance in excess of 'taxable minimum'
	Jobsearch allowances
	Mobility allowance
	One-parent benefit
	Severe disablement allowance
	Employment training allowance
	War orphan's pension
	War widow's pension
	Widow's payment

Fig. 13. Social security benefits.

INCOME *for the year ended 5 April 2000, continued*

Q 11 Did you receive a taxable UK pension, retirement annuity or Social Security benefit?
Read the notes on pages 12 to 14 of the Tax Return Guide.

NO ☐ YES ☐   If yes, fill in boxes 11.1 to 11.13 as appropriate.

■ *State pensions and benefits*   Taxable amount for 1999-2000

- State Retirement Pension (enter the total of your weekly entitlements for the year)   **11.1** £
- Widow's Pension   **11.2** £
- Widowed Mother's Allowance   **11.3** £
- Industrial Death Benefit Pension   **11.4** £
- Jobseeker's Allowance   **11.5** £
- Invalid Care Allowance   **11.6** £
- Statutory Sick Pay and Statutory Maternity Pay paid by the Department of Social Security   **11.7** £

	Tax deducted	Gross amount before tax
• Taxable Incapacity Benefit	**11.8** £	**11.9** £

■ *Other pensions and retirement annuities*

	Amount after tax deducted	Tax deducted	Gross amount before tax
• Pensions (other than State pensions) and retirement annuities	**11.10** £	**11.11** £	**11.12** £

	Amount of deduction
• Deduction - see the note for box 11.13 on page 14 of your Tax Return Guide	**11.13** £

Q 12 Did you receive any of the following kinds of income?

NO ☐ YES ☐   If yes, fill in boxes 12.1 to 12.15 as appropriate.

	Income (taxable)	Exempt amount	Income *minus* exempt amount
• Taxable maintenance or alimony	**12.1** £	**12.2** £	**12.3** £

	Number of years		Amount of gain(s)
• Gains on UK annuities and friendly societies' life insurance policies where tax is treated as paid	**12.4**		**12.5** £

	Number of years	Tax treated as paid	Amount of gain(s)
• Gains on life insurance policies etc. on which tax is treated as paid - read page 15 of the Tax Return Guide	**12.6**	**12.7** £	**12.8** £

	Number of years	Tax deducted	Amount of gain(s)
• Gains on life insurance policies in ISAs that have been made void	**12.9**	**12.10** £	**12.11** £

	Amount
• Corresponding deficiency relief	**12.12** £

	Amount received	Notional tax	Amount plus notional tax
• Refunds of surplus funds from additional voluntary contributions	**12.13** £	**12.14** £	**12.15** £

Q 13 Did you receive any other income which you have not already entered elsewhere in your Tax Return?
Make sure you fill in any supplementary Pages before answering Question 13.

NO ☐ YES ☐   If yes, fill in boxes 13.1 to 13.6 as appropriate.

	Amount after tax deducted	Tax deducted	Amount before tax
• Other income (read page 16 of your Tax Return Guide if you made losses)	**13.1** £	**13.2** £	**13.3** £

	Losses brought forward	Earlier years' losses used in 1999-2000
	13.4 £	**13.5** £

	1999-2000 losses carried forward
	13.6 £

Fig. 14. Page 4 of self assessment tax return.

may, if you wish, calculate the actual income less expenses. This could be particularly useful if you have made a loss, which would be claimable against other property income of the same year; otherwise, it gets carried forward to set against future profits from the same source.

HOW?

If the rents do not exceed £4,250, tick the 'Yes' box of the first question on page 1 of the Land and Property pages of your self-assessment tax return (see Figure 15).

If the rents exceed £4,250, enter the total rents in box 5.20 on page 2 of the Land and Property pages (see Figure 16), and the exempt amount (*ie* £4,250) in box 5.35.

If you wish to enter the actual rents and expenses, enter the gross rents in box 5.20, and the expenses in boxes 5.24 to 5.29, and boxes 5.36, 5.37 of page 2.

Question and answer
If I do bed and breakfast, or run a guest house, can I claim rent-a-room relief on that income?

No. Bed and breakfast or guest house lettings are a commercial enterprise amounting to a trade. They should be declared under the self-employed section or the partnership section of the tax return.

REDUCING EXPENSES OR INCREASING INCOME?

There may be circumstances when you have the option to increase your income or reduce your expenses. Perhaps you receive a bonus or a windfall of some kind. You could invest the money and increase your income, or pay off all or some of your mortgage and thereby reduce your expenses.

If you have used up all the opportunities to get exempt income, the income would be taxable. However, if you reduced your expenses, you would be reducing something which is not taxable, (or at the very most, mortgage interest relief attracting tax relief of 10% only). It is therefore more tax efficient to reduce your expenses.

Question and answer
I have £10,000 in savings, and a £10,000 mortgage. Is it best to pay off the mortgage or leave it in savings?

Income for the year ended 5 April 2000

Inland Revenue

LAND AND PROPERTY

If you have answered 'Yes' to Question 5, fill in Pages L1 and L2. If you want help, look up the box number in the Notes on Land and Property at the back of your Tax Return Guide. They are colour-coded to match the form.

Answer these two questions to help you decide which parts of Pages L1 and L2 to fill in.

Are you claiming Rent a Room relief for gross rents of £4,250 or less?
(Or £2,125 if the claim is shared?)
Read the Notes on page LN2 to find out
- whether you can claim Rent a Room relief; and
- how to claim relief for gross rents over £4,250

No ☐ Yes ☐

If 'Yes', and this is your only income from UK property, you have finished these Pages

Is your income from furnished holiday lettings?
If 'No', turn over and fill in Page L2 to give details of your property income

No ☐ Yes ☐

If 'Yes', fill in boxes 5.1 to 5.18 before completing Page L2

Furnished holiday lettings

- Income from furnished holiday lettings — **5.1** £

■ *Expenses* (furnished holiday lettings only)

- Rent, rates, insurance, ground rents etc. — **5.2** £
- Repairs, maintenance and renewals — **5.3** £
- Finance charges, including interest — **5.4** £
- Legal and professional costs — **5.5** £
- Costs of services provided, including wages — **5.6** £
- Other expenses — **5.7** £

total of boxes 5.2 to 5.7
5.8 £

Net profit (put figures in ~~brackets~~)

box 5.1 *minus* box 5.8
5.9 £

■ *Tax adjustments*

- Private use — **5.10** £
- Balancing charges — **5.11** £

box 5.10 + box 5.11
5.12 £

- Capital allowances — **5.13** £

Profit for the year (copy to box 5.19). If loss, enter '0' in box 5.14 and put the loss in box 5.15

boxes 5.9 + 5.12 *minus* box 5.13
5.14 £

Loss for the year (if you have entered '0' in box 5.14)

boxes 5.9 + 5.12 *minus* box 5.13
5.15 £

■ *Losses*

- Loss offset against 1999-2000 total income — **5.16** £

see Notes, page LN4,
- Loss carried back — **5.17** £

see Notes, page LN4
- Loss offset against other income from property (copy to box 5.38) — **5.18** £

Fig. 15. Land and property pages of tax return: page 1.

Other property income

■ *Income*

• Furnished holiday lettings profits	copy from box 5.14 **5.19** £	
• Rents and other income from land and property	**5.20** £	Tax deducted **5.21** £
• Chargeable premiums	**5.22** £	
• Reverse premiums	**5.22A** £	boxes 5.19 + 5.20 + 5.22 + 5.22A **5.23** £

■ *Expenses* (do not include figures you have already put in boxes 5.2 to 5.7 on Page L1)

• Rent, rates, insurance, ground rents etc.	**5.24** £	
• Repairs, maintenance and renewals	**5.25** £	
• Finance charges, including interest	**5.26** £	
• Legal and professional costs	**5.27** £	
• Costs of services provided, including wages	**5.28** £	
• Other expenses	**5.29** £	total of boxes 5.24 to 5.29 **5.30** £

Net profit (put figures in brackets if a loss) box 5.23 *minus* box 5.30 **5.31** £

■ *Tax adjustments*

• Private use	**5.32** £	
• Balancing charges	**5.33** £	box 5.32 + box 5.33 **5.34** £
• Rent a Room exempt amount	**5.35** £	
• Capital allowances	**5.36** £	
• 10% wear and tear	**5.37** £	
• Furnished holiday lettings losses (from box 5.18)	**5.38** £	total of boxes 5.35 to 5.38 **5.39** £

Adjusted profit (if loss enter '0' in box 5.40 and put the loss in box 5.41) boxes 5.31 + 5.34 *minus* box 5.39 **5.40** £

Adjusted loss (if you have entered '0' in box 5.40) boxes 5.31 + 5.34 *minus* box 5.39 **5.41** £

• Loss brought forward from previous year **5.42** £

Profit for the year box 5.40 *minus* box 5.42 **5.43** £

■ *Losses*

• Loss offset against total income (read the note on page LN8) **5.44** £

• Loss to carry forward to following year **5.45** £

• Pooled expenses from 'one-estate election' carried forward **5.46** £

Tick box 5.47 if these Pages include details of property let jointly **5.47**

Now fill in any other supplementary Pages that apply to you.
Otherwise, go back to page 2 of your Tax Return and finish filling it in.

SPECIMEN

Fig. 16. Land and property pages of tax return: page 2.

The answer depends on your personal circumstances, but you may well feel more comfortable with at least some 'cushion' of savings for an emergency which might occur. You may therefore want to pay off some of the mortgage, and leave yourself with some savings.

Discounts or commissions

If you receive commissions from a company, such as an insurance company, for introducing new business, you may or may not be taxable. It all depends on whether:

● you are receiving the commission for your own business or another person's business (if for another person, whether that person is a relative of yours)

● you are an employee of the company

● you are receiving the same benefit as any other member of the public might get.

However, if you would otherwise be taxable, you might be able to persuade the company to discount your own premiums instead of giving you a commission. This would then not be taxable.

The position may not be the same, however, for a pension policy. If you are offered either a commission or premium discount on your own pension policy, it is normally better to take the commission, particularly if you pay tax at the highest rate. This is because a commission you receive for your own policy is not taxable anyway, whether you are an employee of the company, a self-employed agent, or an ordinary member of the public It is therefore better to pay the full premium and get tax relief of 40% on it. Of course, if the commission you are offered is more than 40%, it is a different matter; but that is not very likely.

EXEMPT ASSETS

Certain assets are exempt from capital gains tax if they are sold at a profit. Remember, though, that if an item is exempt, a loss incurred on disposal of it is not allowable against other gains. Here are some of the most important exemptions.

Government securities

Most government securities are exempt from capital gains tax on any profits made on selling them.

Private residence

If a house or other property is your private residence, any profit on the sale of it is free of capital gains tax. For these purposes, a house includes land which goes with a house, i.e. a garden. The normal limit for size of land is half a hectare (5,980 square yards), but a larger garden can be exempted if required for the reasonable enjoyment of the house, having regard to its size and character.

Partial exemption

If you have owned a house, but it was not your sole private residence for any part of that time, you will only benefit from partial exemption. The part which is exempt is, of course, the time during which it was your sole residence.

Example

You bought a house in April 1992 for £80,000. You sold it in April 2000 for £120,000. During these eight years, you lived in it for four years, then left it empty for the other four years, while you lived in a second house which you bought, and elected as your main residence. The chargeable gain is worked out as follows:

Sale price		120,000
Purchase price	80,000	
Indexation 30%	24,000	
		104,000
Gain		£16,000

The private exemption is 50% (i.e. four years out of eight years). The chargeable gain is therefore £8,000.

There could be also a partial exemption if part of the house had been used exclusively for business purposes. In this case, the proportion of the gain representing the part used exclusively for business purposes is liable to capital gains tax.

Election for main residence

If you have more than one house, and you live in them all, you must make an election for one of them to be the main residence for capital gains tax purposes.

You may also elect for different houses to be your main residence at different periods. If you do this, however, you need to keep good records of what periods you have elected for, since the calculations could become somewhat complicated.

Question and answer
*If I have two houses, and wish to elect for one of them to be my main
residence, does it have to be the one in which I spend most time?*

No. The election for main residence does not necessarily have to be the
one at which you spend the most time. You may elect for the house
which you think will have the most profit to be the main residence for
capital gains tax purposes.

Occupation by dependent relative
If you have a second house that would not otherwise be your main
residence, but you provide it rent free to a dependent relative, then it is
counted as exempt for that period.

Exemption for residential letting
If you let your house out as residential accommodation, the gain which
would otherwise be chargeable is counted as exempt to the extent of the
lower of:

● £40,000 or

● the amount of the gain exempt under normal private residence
rules.

Example
You sold your house in April 2000 and made a gain after indexation of
£60,000. The private residence exemption was one third, i.e. £20,000.
During the time it was not your private residence, you let it out as a
residential letting.

The calculation is as follows:

Gain		60,000
Private exemption		20,000
Chargeable before residential letting exemption		40,000
Less exemption for residential letting –		
The lower of – fixed amount	40,000	
private exemption	20,000	
		20,000
Chargeable		£20,000

HOW?
If the house you have sold is simply the sole private residence, you do not have to declare it on your self assessment tax return. If there is a partial exemption, you must do all the calculations and enter the gross proceeds in column F of page 2 of the capital gains pages of your self assessment tax return (See Figure 11), and the net chargeable amount in the end column.

Chattels
These are defined as 'tangible movable assets' (except commodities disposed of through a dealer on a terminal market). They are exempt from capital gains tax if the disposal proceeds are £6,000 or less. If the disposal proceeds exceed £6,000, the chargeable gain cannot exceed five thirds of the excess over £6,000.

Question and answer
I have a set of items, which together are worth more than £6,000, but individually are worth less than that. Can I dispose of them individually and take advantage of the exemption?

No. Items forming a set are considered as one asset, provided that they are sold to:

● the same person, or

● persons acting together, or

● to a connected person (see Chapter 13).

Debts
A debt disposed of by the original creditor (or his personal representative) is exempt.

Decorations
The disposal of a decoration for valour or gallantry is exempt.

Foreign currency
Disposals of foreign currency are exempt, so long as they were acquired for the individual's personal expenditure while abroad.

Otherwise, currency of any description is not exempt in itself. Note, however, that sovereigns minted before 1838 are not legal tender, and are therefore exempt.

Motor cars
Disposals of motor cars are exempt.

Qualifying corporate bonds
Disposals of these are exempt.

CASE STUDIES

Betty takes full advantage of exempt income
Betty has been widowed for a few years, and has the money her husband left her. It is invested in various types of investment. For some years now, she has been taking advantage of the annual allowances for PEPs, and TESSAs. She will continue to take advantage of ISAs, so that as much as possible of her income is tax free.

Carla pays off her mortgage
Carla has a mortgage of £15,000, when she inherits a lump sum of £30,000 from an aunt.

After taking advice, she decides to pay off the mortgage, and invest the rest. Paying off the mortgage will not only reduce her interest charges, but also the mortgage protection policy she had to take out. She is considerably better off than if she had invested the whole £30,000 and left her mortgage.

PERSONAL TAX EFFICIENCY AUDIT

1. Are you aware of all the tax-free types of savings and other income that are available? Do you feel that any of them fit in with your financial strategy?

2. Are you aware of any exempt assets for capital gains tax purposes? Could you add any of them to your assets, to increase your tax efficiency?

10

Paying Less Inheritance Tax

> In this world, nothing can be said to be certain
> except death and taxes.
>
> Benjamin Franklin

Inheritance tax is one that does not strike until you have died, so it may seem unnecessary to plan to pay less. However, this tax strikes at your dependants. Therefore, unless you really want the Inland Revenue to inherit some of your estate, at the expense of your survivors, you ought to think about this tax.

Inheritance tax is payable on death, at a rate of 40% on any of your estate that exceeds £234,000. The first £234,000 is at a nil rate.

LIFETIME TRANSFERS

There is also a lower rate of tax (20%) on some transfers of assets during your lifetime. The transfers which are caught by this tax are transfers into a discretionary trust. Again, however, the first £234,000 is at a nil rate, and only the excess over £234,000 is taxed at 20%.

A **discretionary trust** is one by which the trustees have discretion to make payments of income out of the trust, and also to decide the shares of the capital of the trust each potential beneficiary will receive.

There is also a periodical tax charge on these trusts every ten years, and an 'exit' tax charge when a distribution of capital is made from the trust.

Inheritance tax on death

The tax is charged on the value of all assets of the deceased, if he or she is domiciled in the UK. If domiciled outside the UK (see Chapter 11), the tax is only charged on assets situated in the UK. It is also charged on gifts or transfers made during the seven years before death. However, assets passing to the spouse of the deceased are exempt from this tax. If you die leaving a spouse, therefore, anything you leave him or her is free of tax. However, anything left to anybody else, including other members of your family, is liable to the tax if your estate is over £234,000.

POTENTIALLY EXEMPT TRANSFERS

Transfers of value can be made without any liability as long as the donor survives seven years after making them. Potentially exempt transfers are any gifts or transfers made to:

● another individual

● an 'Interest in Possession' trust

● an 'Accumulation and Maintenance' trust

● a trust for a mentally or physically disabled person.

Any transfers or gifts not falling within these categories are chargeable transfers.

HOW?

To claim the relief of a potentially exempt transfer, it is important to keep detailed records of your financial transactions. Thus, when you die and your executor comes to sort out your estate, they will have records of the dates and persons to whom you have made transfers.

Tapering the relief

If a person has made one or more potentially exempt transfers, and dies within seven years, the value of the gift or transfer is brought into the estate, but the tax on them is reduced by the following amounts:

Number of complete years since the gift was made	Percentage of tax payable on death
Not more than 3	100
More than 3 but less than 4	80
More than 4 but less than 5	60
More than 5 but less than 6	40
More than 6 but less than 7	20
More than 7	NIL

However, this relief is largely illusory. If the gift is below the £234,000 limit, the tapering relief is effectively zero.

EXEMPT TRANSFERS

Apart from the potentially exempt transfers, some transfers or gifts are exempt without any qualification. These can therefore be used as a tool to pay less inheritance tax. The exempt transfers are as follows:

Transfers between husband and wife
We have already seen that anything passing between husband and wife at death is exempt. Anything passing between husband and wife during their lifetime is also exempt. There are two of points to note, however.

1. This exemption only applies to husband and wife. Unmarried people living together do not qualify for this exemption, even if one is wholly dependent on the other.

2. If the recipient of the gift or transfer is not domiciled in the UK, the exemption is limited to £55,000.

Annual exemption
Everybody is allowed to give away £3,000 each tax year free of inheritance tax. Further, if you do not use up this exemption in one tax year, it can be carried forward and used the next year. However, this carry forward is only valid for one year. It cannot be carried forward any more than one year.

Small gifts exemption
Everybody may give away as many outright gifts as they like in a tax year, up to a total of £250 for each receiver of these gifts. Any gift over £250 is not exempt on the whole amount – not just the excess over £250.

Wedding gifts
You may make wedding gifts free of inheritance tax to either the bride or the groom. These gifts are exempt up to certain limits depending on the relationship between the giver and the receiver, as follows:

A parent	£5,000
A grandparent or great-grandparent	£2,500
Anyone else	£1,000

The bride and groom can also give each other wedding gifts before the wedding up to £2,500 each. After the wedding, of course, all gifts and transfers are exempt, because they are between husband and wife.

Normal expenditure from income
Any regular gifts made from income are exempt, provided that they do not reduce the usual standard of living, and that they are made out of income, not capital.

To qualify for this exemption, it is usually necessary to establish a pattern of gifts, over a period of years. It is also necessary to be able to prove that the gifts were made out of income, not capital.

Family maintenance gifts
Gifts made for the maintenance of a spouse, child or dependent relative are exempt. This definition includes illegitimate children, stepchildren and adopted children.

Gifts to political parties and charities
Gifts of any amount to registered charities and the main political parties are exempt from tax – whether made during your lifetime, or as part of your will.

HOW?

Once again, the key to getting relief for exempt transfers is to keep as full a record as possible. This is particularly important if there is the possibility of establishing a regular pattern of gifts for the 'normal expenditure from income' exemption.

PLANNING FOR INHERITANCE TAX

Planning for inheritance tax involves decisions which sometimes extend beyond merely financial considerations. These decisions are often very personal by nature, and frequently involve your family – both close family and more distant relatives. Therefore, it is a good idea to discuss these plans at least with your most immediate family.

Also, these decisions, more than any other related to tax saving, are likely to benefit from consultation with professionals – tax advisers or solicitors.

Finally, whatever the government in power, the earlier you make these decisions, the better.

Basic considerations

When making any plans to save inheritance tax, you must always ensure that you, or your potential widow or widower, have enough income to live on as comfortably as possible. It is no use living in tax efficient poverty! For this reason, planning earlier in your life for an adequate pension is important. It means that there will be less pressure to hold on to assets later in life because they are needed to generate an income.

SHARING ASSETS

As a general rule of thumb, husbands and wives should normally share their assets as equally as they can. This is useful not only for inheritance tax, but also for other taxes. Each spouse can then make full use of the exemptions and the nil rate band.

Question and answer
Is it always beneficial to divide assets equally between husband and wife?

This is normally the general rule. Assets are better shared equally. However, there may be circumstances when one spouse does not want to relinquish a hold on part of the assets. This is particularly noticeable if the marriage itself is not stable.

MAKING A WILL

Apart from the administrative difficulties, not leaving a will can cost your survivors. A will should take into account the inheritance tax liability and the way it strikes.

For instance, if all your estate is left to your spouse, that could be a missed opportunity. This is because all transfers between husband and wife are exempt anyway. Therefore, you could leave an amount up the limit of the nil rate band (currently £234,000) to the next generation, or other beneficiaries, without any liability.

Again, it must be emphasised that this must only be done if there is adequate money for the surviving spouse to live on. Also, it is not worth passing down more than the nil rate band, because it would mean paying inheritance tax earlier than necessary.

It may be possible for the surviving beneficiaries to agree on a 'deed of variation' within two years of the death. This can take effect as if the terms were written in the original will. However, a recent court case has created inheritance tax problems for certain variations. It is always best to have a properly drafted will in the first place.

USING LIFE ASSURANCE

This is particularly useful for married couples. The inheritance tax charge normally comes on the second death. A life assurance policy written in trust for the survivors can play an important role in providing the funds to pay the inheritance tax. If a policy is written in trust, the proceeds on the second death are outside the estate, and therefore do not count towards the estate on which the tax is charged. If it is written on the joint lives, to pay out on the second death, the premium is normally much lower. If a couple start paying the premiums early in their lives, the premiums will normally be much lower, and the premiums can become part of their normal expenditure from income and thereby an exempt transfer.

USING TRUSTS

As we have seen, trusts are a technical area for which you will need the advice and help of a solicitor. Discretionary trusts are the most flexible, since the trustee has absolute discretion to distribute the income and capital. If you give money into a trust you may also be a trustee, so you may retain control over the money given into the trust while it is outside your estate. However, as we have seen earlier in this chapter, discretionary trusts do suffer tax charges before you die.

Other types of trust

An **accumulation and maintenance trust** is normally set up for children or grandchildren. Money given by you into an accumulation and maintenance trust is a potentially exempt transfer. There is therefore no immediate tax charge, and none at all if you survive seven years. Under this type of trust, the income must be accumulated for the child until they reach an age between 18 and 25. However, the trustee may distribute income from the trust for the maintenance and education of the children. In order to qualify for the potentially exempt status, the trust must:

● have beneficiaries who are all grandchildren of a common grand-parent, and are aged under 25 at the time the trust is made

● ensure that the beneficiaries become entitled to the income of the trust at age 25 at the latest (the capital may pass at a later date)

● accumulate any income not applied to the maintenance or education of the beneficiaries.

An **interest in possession** trust is one by which certain beneficiaries may enjoy the income of the trust for their lifetime; on their death, the capital of the trust is paid out according to the wishes of the person who made the trust. If the person who gives the money into this type of trust is also a trustee, he or she may vary the way in which the income of the trust is distributed while he or she is alive.

Whichever type of trust is made, it does have the benefit of being able to protect the assets. If the trust is properly worded, it can protect assets from divorce, creditors, or predatory step-relatives. It can even protect the assets from the beneficiary while that beneficiary is young or immature.

MAKING GIFTS

You may take advantage of gifts during your lifetime to reduce the ultimate inheritance tax liability on your estate. The combined effect of the nil rate band and the seven-year cumulative rule for potentially exempt transfers can often go a long way to mitigating this tax. Gifts do not, of course, have to be made in money, but they can be any other assets. When deciding what assets to give, think about their future potential. The value of the gift for these purposes is the value of the gift at the time it is given. Therefore, it is more tax efficient to give a gift that is likely to increase in value. This way, any increase in value of that asset comes outside your estate.

If, for example, you have a property that is let to an elderly person, that property would increase in value when the tenant dies. (An empty property is always worth more than a tenanted one).

There are two points to remember, however:

1. Firstly, the gift must be given outright. There must be no 'reservation of benefit'. For instance, if you gave your house to your children, but carried on living in it without paying the full market rent, that would be a gift with reservation of benefit. Any such gifts are not potentially exempt transfers. They are still counted as part of your estate when you die.

2. Secondly, you should not give away more than you can afford. It is no use leaving your survivors free of inheritance tax if the price is that you live in poverty for the rest of your life. This point has been made already, but it is worth repeating.

MAKING USE OF BUSINESS PROPERTY RELIEF AND AGRICULTURAL PROPERTY RELIEF

There are some very valuable reliefs for businesses and agricultural land.

Business property relief

Business property relief at 100%

● the business of a sole trader or the interest of a partner in the partnership business

● shareholdings in a trading company that is not quoted on a recognised stock exchange.

Business property relief at 50%

● shares or securities giving control of a trading company that is quoted on a recognised stock exchange

● land and buildings, machinery or equipment which:
  - you own, or
  - a trust of which you are a beneficiary owns, but used by a trading company under your control, or a partnership in which you are a partner.

There are important conditions attached to the business property relief:

1. You must have owned the property at least two years before the gift or death.

2. The company or business must be a trading business. The relief does not apply to investment companies. Nor does it apply to non-business assets. The relief can be restricted if any of the assets have not been used mainly for business purposes.

3. There must be no binding agreement in force for the sale of your interest in the business.

4. If an asset qualifying for this relief is given as a potentially exempt transfer, it must still be owned by the original recipient and still qualify as a business asset at the date of death, if death occurs within seven years.

Agricultural property relief

This relief is given on the agricultural value of land and farm buildings occupied for agriculture. For these purposes, agriculture includes forestry, fish farming, stud farming and intensive livestock rearing.

Agricultural property relief at 100%

● land on which you have farmed for at least the last two years, or where you can obtain vacant possession within 24 months

● land farmed by a tenant under a lease that started after 31 August 1995; you, the owner, cannot obtain vacant possession of the land within one year. You must have owned the land for at least seven years, and it must have been farmed for all that period.

Agricultural property relief at 50%

● land farmed by a tenant under a lease that started before 1 September 1995, with the same conditions as above.

There are also conditions applying to this relief.

1. Not all the assets of the farm qualify as agricultural property. The farmhouse is disallowed, and outlying 'amenity' woodland may also not be allowed.

2. Where agricultural property relief and business property relief are both available, the agricultural property relief is given first. Most assets in a farming business will qualify for business property relief, even if they do not qualify for agricultural property relief.

3. If any part of a farm has development value, that land will qualify for agricultural property relief on the agricultural value, and business property relief will most likely apply to the enhanced development value.

4. You are treated as occupying land if you are a partner in a partnership which farms the land, or you control a company which farms the land. Therefore, a transfer of shares in a company which you control, and which farms the land, may qualify.

5. If you die within seven years of making a potentially exempt transfer which qualified for agricultural property relief, the land must still be owned by the original recipient and still qualify as agricultural land for the relief to apply.

Planning for Business Property and Agricultural Property Relief

The rules, as we have seen, are fairly complex. You should be careful about making sure you comply with them. For example:

- Make sure that the qualifying periods of ownership apply if you make a transfer or gift of business or agricultural property. In particular, if there has been a transfer between husband and wife, make sure the qualifying period is adhered to after the first transfer.

- The provision about a binding contract for sale is important. If you are in a partnership, therefore, make sure that there is no clause in the partnership agreement which states that, on the death of a partner, 'the surviving partners shall acquire the share of the deceased partner at market value'. It may, however, say that the surviving partners have the option to buy the share of the deceased partner at market value.

- An asset qualifying for business property relief or agricultural property relief is reduced by any loans secured on that asset. Therefore, if there is a mortgage on business property, the value qualifying for 100% or 50% exemption is reduced by the outstanding mortgage. It is obviously better, therefore, if a mortgage could be secured on non-business property – say, the domestic residence.

- If a company has been carrying out property development, it qualifies for business property relief. However, if properties do not sell, and they are let, that counts as investment income, i.e. nontrading income. The relief could therefore be lost or reduced.

CASE STUDIES

Dennis and Maggie revise their wills

Dennis and Maggie are well into retirement, and quite well off. They have a son and a daughter, and several grandchildren. The subject of their inheritance tax plans has been sparked off by the marriage of the first of their grandchildren. They take advantage straight away of the exemption and give a wedding gift to their grandson of £2,500. They then feel that they could well afford to give away certain other gifts without prejudicing their standard of living. They have not used up their annual exemption this tax year or last year, so they can give away up to £12,000 between them. They give £4,000 to each of their two children, and £1,000 to each of their remaining four grandchildren.

They then give some attention to their wills. They amend their wills so as to leave £200,000 (almost the extent of the nil rate band) amongst their children and grandchildren. They leave the rest of their estates to each other. They had already equalised their estates as far as practicable in a previous exercise. The house is held jointly, and their investments are held more or less equally. Even after giving £200,000 away on the first death, the survivor will have an adequate income. There would then be a small amount of inheritance tax to pay, but they reckon that they have done enough now substantially to ease the burden of inheritance tax.

Neil and Glenys pay a life assurance premium

Neil and Glenys are also fairly well off, but not so well off as Dennis and Maggie. Having considered their inheritance tax position, they decide to take out a life assurance policy written in trust for their survivors (they have three children and three grandchildren). The policy is written for the benefit to become payable on the second death. The policy is for the current estimated amount of inheritance tax which would be payable. The premium is comfortably affordable, and comes within their annual exemption.

They do not amend their wills. They have left everything to each other, so that the inheritance tax liability will only apply on the second death.

PERSONAL TAX EFFICIENCY AUDIT

1. Do you and your spouse have wills? Are they regularly revised in the light of changing circumstances?

2. Have you passed on as much as you want your children and grandchildren to have before your death?

3. Do you make full use of the exempt transfers?

4. How are your assets divided between you and your spouse? Could they be better divided for inheritance tax purposes?

5. Have you considered the use of trusts or life assurance policies?

11

Becoming a Tax Exile

The most difficult thing in the world to understand
is income tax.

Albert Einstein

Living abroad has a romantic ring about it, conjuring up visions of an
idyllic lifestyle on a tropical beach. Certainly it is usually associated
with film stars, pop stars and the whole glamorous world that
accompanies them. What is the reality behind it?

WEIGHING UP THE PROS AND CONS

Even if your income is such that you are seriously considering
becoming a tax exile, there are other, non-financial, matters to bear in
mind. You must become resigned, above all, to not being in the UK for
certain times. You may not be able to plan all the occasions when you
would like to return to this country. There may be unforeseen
circumstances, family crises or other events.

Quite apart from the patriotic aspect, there is the simple matter of
having to monitor your movements. You must be quite sure that you will
be happy living in the country of your choice. Many people enjoy the
initial 'honeymoon' period, but disillusionment settles in after a while.
And, of course, you need to be sure that you will not be taxed more
heavily in the country to which you go.

THE BASIC RULES

The basic rules are:

- If you are resident in the UK for any tax year, you are liable to UK
  tax on all of your income and gains whether they are from UK or
  overseas sources.

- If you are non-resident in the UK, you are only liable to income
  from sources in the UK.

- If you are not domiciled in the UK, but you are resident in the UK, you are liable to tax on overseas income only to the extent that it is remitted to the UK.

- If you are resident in the UK but not ordinarily resident, then you are only liable to UK tax on income remitted to this country.

UNDERSTANDING THE CONCEPTS

Your tax liability in this country may be dependent on your residence, your ordinary residence, or your domicile. You may be resident in this country, but not domiciled in this country. You may be resident but not ordinarily resident. You may even be resident in more than one country for tax purposes.

Residence

Strangely, there is very little actual statutory guidance on the definition of residence in the tax laws of this country. The concept of residence is largely one of actual physical presence in this country. When you are resident in this country for six months or more during a tax year, then you are resident for tax purposes.

It you leave this country to work abroad full time, you are treated as non-resident, so long as the following conditions are met (and the Inland Revenue have indicated that they will accept that a self-employed businessman or woman working abroad meeting similar conditions is also non-resident).

- You must not visit this country for more than 182 days in the tax year, and

- your visits to this country averaged over four years do not exceed an average of 90 days per year, and

- you must be working full-time abroad under a contract of employment (not necessarily with an overseas company)

- you must be abroad (apart from the visits to this country) for the whole of the tax year concerned. Thus, you cannot be considered non-resident if you were abroad from 1 July to 30 June the following year. There is not full tax year involved here. (The tax year, of course, runs from 6 April to the following 5 April.).

If you leave the country permanently, you are treated as non-resident if you do not visit this country for more than 90 days each year. If you retain accommodation in this country, you must produce evidence of some sort that your emigration from this country is permanent. Steps taken to acquire a permanent home abroad are the most convincing evidence.

Ordinary residence

This term is not defined anywhere in the tax laws of this country. It signifies a greater permanence, and is normally decided by habitual residence. You will normally be regarded as ordinarily resident if:

● you visit this country regularly, and

● you have accommodation available in this country, or

● your visits average more than 90 days per year (ignoring days in this country for circumstances beyond your control, such as illness of yourself or a family member).

Domicile

This is a different concept from residence. It is the country you consider as your permanent home. You acquire a domicile of origin at birth (normally the domicile of your father). You may then change this to a domicile of choice, determined by your subsequent actions, including marriage and/or emigration.

Foreign earnings deduction

There is now no general deduction for foreign earnings. There used to be a 100% exemption for earnings from an overseas job provided that it lasted more than one year. Now, the non-resident conditions have to be met.

Benefiting from non-residence

If you are non-resident, you are not liable to tax in this country on any income arising abroad. Income arising in this country is, however, subject to tax. If you are a UK citizen, you are entitled to the personal allowances available, including the married couple's allowance.

By concession from the Inland Revenue, a person married to a person who has a full-time job abroad, and who accompanies their spouse, can benefit from the same non-resident status as their spouse. This is on the basis of the spouse's movements and employment, not their own.

If a person working abroad full-time, and qualifying for the non-resident status, is not accompanied by their spouse, they can transfer any unused married couple's allowance to the spouse who is still in this country.

Capital gains tax and non-residence

If you are not resident in this country for the whole of a tax year, then any capital gain you make in that tax year is not liable to capital gains tax. However, if you return to the UK before having been non-resident for five full tax years, then you will be liable to capital gains on any gains you made while non-resident, if you owned those assets at the time of your departure from this country.

CASE STUDIES

Bill and Hilary consider emigration

Bill and Hilary are very wealthy, and have a very high income. After consultation with their tax lawyer and accountant, they seriously consider the possibility of living abroad for tax purposes. First, they decide that if they did, they would both have to go together. They could not stand the separation of living in different countries. Then they consider the various family matters, and discuss them with their family. At first, their children (now all grown up) respond positively to the idea of being able to visit their parents on some tropical paradise island. But the children have second thoughts when they go home and think about it.

In the end, Bill and Hilary decide to stay here. They still feel that their family ties, with grandchildren, and various cousins and uncles and aunts, are stronger than the merely financial aspects. In addition, they realise that although they may save tax, they are already well off, even after paying tax. Enough is as good as a feast, they decide, and stay in this country.

PERSONAL TAX EFFICIENCY AUDIT

1. Are your affairs complex enough, or is your income in a high enough bracket, to consider becoming a tax exile?

2. If your job takes you abroad, have you discussed with your employer the tax position, and have you worked out the dates you will need to cover to take advantage of any exemptions for non-residence?

12

Avoiding Penalties, Interest and Surcharges

It would be particularly ironic if, having saved tax through the various means outlined in this book, you were to incur penalties, interest or surcharges. These are extra charges which can be avoided by complying with all the legal requirements, and ensuring that all forms, etc. are dealt with inside the time limits laid down.

OBSERVING TIME LIMITS

Sending in tax returns
One of the most obvious and important deadlines is that for filing your self-assessment tax return. If you want the Inspector of Taxes to carry out the calculations, you must get the return in by the later of:

● 30 September after the end of the tax year, or

● two months after the tax return has been sent to you.

If you miss this deadline, there is no penalty, but you must do your own calculations. The final deadline is the later of:

● 31 January after the end of the tax year, or

● three months after the tax return has been sent to you.

If you miss this last deadline, there an automatic penalty of £100. The Inspector of Taxes will send you a notice of penalty. If it is more than six months late, the penalty is increased to £200.

If the Commissioners have directed that the tax return must be sent in, the Inspector of Taxes may ask the Commissioners to apply a further penalty of £60 per day after the direction is made. The Inland Revenue have indicated that they will only seek to apply this particular penalty when the tax at risk is believed to be high.

If the tax return is still outstanding a year after the normal last filing date, a further penalty of up to 100% of the tax liability may be imposed.

The total of all these penalties is limited to the amount of tax due.

HOW?

If you receive a penalty notice, you must pay the amount. A payslip is attached to the notice for you to make your payment. As noted below, you may make an appeal, but the Inland Revenue always recommend that you pay the amount due. If the appeal decision goes against you, you have paid the amount due, and there will be no interest added. If the appeal is successful, you will be repaid, with interest if applicable.

You may appeal to the Commissioners against these penalties. They may be set aside if you can show that you had a reasonable excuse for the delay. The reasonable excuse must have applied throughout the whole period of failure, not just for part of the period.

HOW?

Write to your Inspector of Taxes, to tell him about your intention to appeal. The case will be listed for hearing before the commissioners, and you will be sent a notice of the date and place of the hearing. You will have to put over your side of the argument, unless you are represented.

PAYING TAX ON TIME

Income tax and capital gains tax due under self assessment have specific deadlines for payment of the tax. These dates are 31 January and 31 July each year. The way in which these payments are calculated is dealt with in more detail in my book *Coping with Self Assessment* (How To Books Ltd).

Question and answer
What do I do if I believe that the amount of tax demanded is wrong?

Write to your Inspector of Taxes to tell him why you disagree, and pay the amount you think should be payable.

Interest

The Inland Revenue send you reminders shortly before each payment of tax is due. If any payment is made late, there is an automatic interest charge on the overdue tax. Interest is charged at the 'official rate' published by the Inland Revenue. A list of the official rates of interest, and the dates to which they applied, is available from your local tax office.

You are sent a 'statement of account' whenever there is tax due, and this shows all tax due, plus any interest, penalties, or surcharges due. Interest accrues automatically on any overdue amounts on the statement.

Surcharges

In addition to interest on overdue tax, the following surcharges are added:

- tax paid after 28 days of due date, but not later than six months – 5% of tax due

- tax paid more than six months after due date – 10% of tax due.

Appeals are allowed against these surcharges, but not against the interest. To set aside the surcharge, you must show a reasonable excuse for late payment. Inability to pay is not accepted as a reasonable excuse.

Surcharges do not apply to payments on account, only to final payments of tax and class 4 National Insurance. A surcharge cannot be imposed in addition to a tax geared penalty.

VAT PENALTIES

There are numerous penalties, surcharges and interest charges for VAT mistakes. Here are some of the more common ones.

Default surcharge

VAT returns are due within a month of the last day of the VAT period. If you are late sending in your VAT return, you are liable to a 'default surcharge'. This is the greater of:

- £30, and

- 2% of the VAT due for the first default

- 5% of the VAT due for the second default

- 10% of the VAT due for the third default

- 15% of the VAT due for the fourth and subsequent default.

The default surcharge, however, is only payable when the Customs and Excise issue a surcharge liability notice specifying a surcharge period. This period effectively is a year from the first late delivery of a return.

What this all means is that if you send in a late return, you are not charged a surcharge if you send your next returns in on time for a period of a year. But if you are late again within a year, you are liable for the default surcharge.

Misdeclaration penalty

If you make a misdeclaration of VAT in a return, you could be liable to a penalty. However, if you discover a mistake and put it right in a subsequent return, no penalty applies. The penalty is 15% of the tax which would have been lost if the inaccuracy had not been discovered.

This sort of mistake is usually found in the course of a VAT inspection by a VAT officer. Therefore, once you have been informed of a VAT inspection, you cannot then declare an error in a past return to avoid the misdeclaration penalty.

Persistent misdeclaration penalty

If you make at least three mistakes in VAT returns of a 'material amount', then the penalty is 15% of the tax which would have been lost if the second and subsequent misdeclarations had not been discovered. The 'material amount' is the lesser of:

● £50,000, and

● 10% of the gross amount of output tax and input tax added together.

Failure to register for VAT

If you should have registered for VAT but have failed to do so, there are penalties. These are the greater of:

● £50 and

● 5% of the tax lost if the failure goes on for nine months or less, or

● 10% of the tax lost if the failure goes on for more than nine months but less than 18 months, or

● 15% of the tax lost if the failure goes on for more than 18 months.

Unauthorised issue of tax invoices

If you issue an invoice purporting to show VAT, but you are not registered, the penalty is the greater of:

- £50, and

- 15% of the amount shown as VAT.

Default interest

If you have not made a return, or the Customs and Excise for any other reason issue an assessment on you, default interest is payable at the official rate (which has been 6.25% from 6 February 1996) on the VAT due under the assessment from the last date on which the VAT return could have been made for the period concerned, up to the date the VAT due on the assessment is paid.

Question and answer
Is there any appeal procedure against VAT penalties?

Yes. You make your appeal to the Customs and Excise office. They list the case for hearing before the VAT tribunal, an independent body. You will be notified of the date and place of the hearing, and you will have to present your case, unless you are represented.

CASE STUDIES

Tony leaves his tax return too late

Tony has been busy, and during the Christmas holidays realises that there is only just over a month to go to get his tax return in. He tries his best to get all the information together, but one source keeps him waiting. At last he gets all the entries together and put in the tax return late at night on 31 January. He takes the tax return to the tax office himself on 1 February. However, he is too late, and he gets a penalty notice of £100. He realises that the fault has been his, so does not try to appeal. He pays the penalty, a poorer but wiser man.

Debbie is hospitalised

Debbie also realises during the Christmas holidays that her tax return should be sent in soon. She writes off to get all the information she can straight away. She is still waiting for it on 15 January when she has a serious car accident. She is in hospital for a month, and can only finish her tax return when she gets home. Although it is sent in late, and the Inland Revenue send a penalty notice, she appeals because of the hospitalisation. Her appeal is successful, and she is excused the penalty. However, she determines that she will start her preparations earlier next year.

PERSONAL TAX EFFICIENCY AUDIT

1. Are you sufficiently organised to start preparing your tax return in good time?

2. Have you set aside the right amount to pay your tax when it becomes due? Are you going to be tempted to use that money for another purpose?

3. If your business has made mistakes in VAT returns, have you investigated the reason for those mistakes? Have you taken steps to ensure that they do not happen again?

13

Avoiding the Pitfalls

Understandably, the Inland Revenue and the Customs and Excise do not take kindly to cheating. There are regulations covering the two main areas where they stop unfair manipulation of the system.

These two areas are **artificial schemes** and **connected persons**.

Artificial schemes are targeted with a range of anti-avoidance provisions. Connected persons legislation governs transactions between connected persons and how they are treated for tax purposes.

ANTI-AVOIDANCE PROVISIONS

On the whole, these provisions arise in response to schemes that are dreamed up by people trying to find loopholes or ways around the law.

There are various cases which have been decided over the years on the way in which certain transactions are taxed. The judgements given in these cases often contain general guidance which is treated by the Inland Revenue as guidelines within which they are able to work.

One of the earliest and most important cases was the Duke of Westminster v CIR. In this, the judge's summing up included the statement that 'every man is entitled if he can to order his affairs so that the tax attaching is less than it would otherwise be'. A later case (W T Ramsay Ltd v CIR) concerned a complicated series of transactions. At the end of these transactions, all parties to the transactions were in the same position as at the beginning, and the transactions were therefore said to be 'circular'. However, in the course of the transactions, a large capital loss had been created. The principle which the judge laid down there was that, where a preconceived series of transactions is entered into to avoid tax, and with the clear intention to proceed through all stages of the transactions at the outset, then the transactions should not be considered in isolation. The commercial reality at the end of the transactions should override the individual transactions taken in isolation.

The later case of Furniss v Dawson extended the Ramsay case. This laid down that the series of transactions need not be 'circular' devices, but any particular transaction within a series of pre-ordained transactions could be ignored if the sole reason for it was for tax avoidance, without any other commercial motive.

What all this means is that if someone offers you a part in a complicated deal purely to save tax, it could be challenged in the courts.

Specific anti-avoidance legislation

There are specific provisions of various Tax Acts to counteract different types of artificial transaction. These deal with the following areas (amongst others) for income tax purposes:

● transactions in securities (e.g. stocks, shares, etc). These cover such things as:

  – abnormal dividends or distributions from companies to shareholders

  – sales of securities with arrangements to repurchase sales of the right to dividends direct sales and repurchases

  – securities held for one month or less

  – 'manufactured' dividends

● transfers of assets abroad, and the right to receive income on those assets

● trading transactions at other than market price, if a non-resident is involved, or the person holds the item traded as a fixed asset

● capital sums in lieu of earnings

● transactions in land – whether the profit is liable to income tax or capital gains tax

● land sold and leased back. Where this happens, the allowance against profits for rent is limited to the commercial market value of the rent. Also, a proportion of the capital sum received for the sale could be taxed

● sale and leaseback of assets other than land. The capital sum received could be taxable

● loss relief on dealing in commodity futures is not given where there is a partnership which includes a company as a partner, and the main benefit expected from the partnership is setting off loss relief from trading against other income.

In addition, there are anti-avoidance provisions for capital gains tax purposes, covering such things as:

- value shifting, including company reorganisations
- company reconstructions and amalgamations
- groups of companies.

The above does not give an exhaustive treatment of the anti-avoidance rules, but it does give some idea of the types of schemes that have been thought up, and the laws necessary to combat these schemes.

CONNECTED PERSONS

The Inland Revenue take the view that transactions between connected persons are not 'at arm's length'. The general principle is that any transactions between connected persons should be treated as if they were made at a normal market value. If you are involved in a 'connected persons' transaction, the onus is on you to justify what the normal market value would be for the transaction carried out.

So who are 'connected persons'?

An **individual** is connected with:

- a spouse
- a brother or brother-in-law
- a sister or sister-in-law
- a parent or parent-in-law
- a grandparent or grandparent-in-law
- a child or child-in-law
- a grandchild or grandchild-in-law.

A **trustee** is connected with:

- the settlor of the trust
- any person connected with the settlor
- any company connected with the settlement.

If you are a **partner** in a business, you are connected with your partners and their spouses and relatives (brothers, sisters, ancestors or lineal descendants).

A **company** is connected with another company if:

- the same person controls both companies, or
- one company is controlled by a person who has control of the other company in conjunction with persons connected with him or her, or
- one person controls one company and a person connected with him or her controls the other company, or
- the same group of persons controls both companies, or
- the companies are controlled by separate groups which can be regarded as the same by interchanging connected persons.

A company is connected with a person who has control of it.

Persons acting together to secure or exercise control of a company are treated in relation to that company as connected to each other.

Question and answer
If I am about to do a transaction with a connected person, what steps should I take to make sure it does not fall foul of the taxman?

If the price of the transaction is different to the open-market value, you should make sure of what the true open-market value is. You would then be taxed on the transaction as if that open-market value were applied.

HOW?

In order to ensure complete transparency of your dealings with the Inland Revenue, you should write in the space for 'additional information' on page 8 of your self assessment tax return (see Figure 17) the details of any connected persons transactions.

PERSONAL TAX EFFICIENCY AUDIT

1. Are you considering any 'schemes' to avoid tax liability? If so, have they been cleared by the Inland Revenue, or tested in the courts?

2. Do you know how to obtain open-market valuations if you are doing any transactions with connected persons?

OTHER INFORMATION *for the year ended 5 April 2000, continued*

Q 22 Please tick boxes 22.1 to 22.5 if they apply and provide any additional information in the box below.

Tick box 22.1 if you expect to receive a new pension or Social Security benefit in 2000-2001. **22.1**

Tick box 22.2 if you do **not** want any tax you owe for 1999-2000 collected through your tax code. **22.2**

Tick box 22.3 if this Tax Return contains figures that are provisional because you do not yet have final figures. Page 27 of your Tax Return Guide explains the circumstances in which Tax Returns containing provisional figures may be accepted and tells you what you must enter in the box below. **22.3**

box number 22.4 is not used

Tick box 22.5 if you want to claim:

- relief now for 2000-2001 trading or certain capital losses. Enter the amount and year in the 'Additional information' box below

- to have post-cessation or other business receipts taxed as income of an earlier year. Enter the amount and year in the 'Additional information' box below

- backwards or forwards spreading of literary or artistic income. Enter in the 'Additional information' box details of any amounts spread back to last year and, if appropriate, the year before

- for a payment to your employer's compulsory widow's, widower's or orphan's benefit scheme (available in some circumstances – read the notes on page 27 of your Tax Return Guide **before** you tick the box). Enter the amount, in terms of tax, in the 'Additional information' box below. **22.5**

Additional information

SPECIMEN

Q 23 Declarat...

I have filled i... ...m sending back to you the following pages:

Tick

| 1 TO 8 OF THIS FORM |
| EMPLOYMENT |
| SHARE SCHEMES |
| SELF-EMPLOYMENT |

Tick

| PARTNERSHIP |
| LAND & PROPERTY |
| FOREIGN |

Tick

| TRUSTS ETC |
| CAPITAL GAINS |
| NON-RESIDENCE ETC |

Before you send your completed Tax Return back to your Inland Revenue office, you must sign the statement below. If you give false information or conceal any part of your income or chargeable gains, you may be liable to financial penalties and/or you may be prosecuted.

23.1 The information I have given in this Tax Return is correct and complete to the best of my knowledge and belief.

Signature   Date

If you have signed for someone else, please also:

- state the capacity in which you are signing (for example, as executor or receiver)

23.2

- give the name of the person you are signing for and **your** name and address in the 'Additional information' box above.

Fig. 17. Page 8 of self assessment tax return.

Glossary

Accumulation and maintenance trust. Special type of trust normally set up for children or grandchildren.

Additional personal allowance. Allowance given to a person not married or not living with their spouse, who is bringing up a child.

Age allowances. The higher allowances given to people over 65.

Agricultural property relief. A relief against inheritance tax for agricultural land.

Allowances. Amounts given as a right as deductions from your income for tax purposes.

Anti-avoidance provisions. Tax laws to prevent unfair advantage being taken of 'loopholes' by taxpayers.

Blind person's allowance. Allowance given to a person registered as blind.

Business property relief. A relief against inheritance tax for business assets.

Capital allowances. Allowances given for the use of assets.

Capital gains tax. A tax on profits made on disposing of assets.

Car benefit. A charge to tax on the value of a car used privately.

Chattels. Tangible moveable assets enjoying capital gains tax exemption.

Charitable covenants. A legally binding document giving tax relief to a charity.

Connected persons. People or companies connected to each other so that transactions between them are not 'at arm's length'.

Corporation tax. The tax charged on companies.

Customs and Excise. The body which administers the assessment and collection of customs duty, excise duties and VAT.

Default surcharge. VAT penalty imposed for late submission of returns.

Discretionary trust. A trust giving the trustee discretion to make payments.

Dividend. An amount paid to shareholders of companies as reward.

Domicile. Permanent status of a person's long-term residence.

Enterprise investment scheme. Special type of investment attracting tax relief.

Extra statutory concessions. Concessions published by the Inland Revenue allowing beneficial tax treatment of various items.

Fuel scale charges. A charge to tax on fuel provided for private use.

Gift aid. A way of making tax-efficient gifts to charities.

ISA. Individual savings account. Type of tax-free savings.

Inheritance tax. Tax due on the transfer of assets from a person – usually on death.

Inland Revenue. The body which administers tax assessment and collection.

Input tax. VAT tax suffered by a business on purchases.

Limited company. A legally constituted company having its own legal identity.

Lower-rate bands. Bands of income taxed at lower rates.

Maintenance or alimony. Relief given for maintenance or alimony payments.

Marginal rate of tax. The effective rate of tax on the highest slice of income.

Married couple's allowance. The allowance given to married couples living together.

MIRAS. Mortgage interest relief given at source.

Misdeclaration penalty. Financial penalty for incorrect declaration of VAT due.

Output tax. VAT on a business's outputs, or sales.

Partnership. A body of persons carrying on business together with a view to profit.

Penalties. Financial fines imposed for non-compliance with tax regulations.

Persistent misdeclaration penalty. Financial penalty for repeated incorrect declaration of VAT due.

Personal allowance. The basic allowance given to everybody for income tax.

Personal equity plan. Tax-free type of investment replaced by ISA.

Personal pension relief. Relief given for premiums paid to an approved pension scheme.

Potentially exempt transfer. Transfer from a person's estate which becomes exempt if the transferor survives seven years.

Residence. Status of a person relating to their place of residence – for tax purposes your status can be UK resident or non-UK resident.

Restricted allowances. Allowances which are restricted by reference to income level.

Retirement relief. A relief given against capital gains tax on retirement from a business.

SAYE. Save as you earn – tax-exempt type of savings plan.

Settlement. A trust. Money or assets transferred by one person to trustees, to be held and applied as directed by the settlor.

Stamp duty. A tax levied on the value of transfer of certain assets.

Surcharges. Financial penalties added to tax due for late payment.

Tapering relief. A relief given against capital gains tax. Also applied to the reduction in the value of potentially exempt transfers if the transferor dies within seven years.

Tax credits. Credits for tax deducted at source from investments.

TESSA. Tax-exempt special savings account.

Transitional allowance. An allowance given when separate taxation for married women was introduced. It is gradually dying out.

Value added tax. Abbreviated to VAT. A tax on business output.

Venture capital trusts. Special type of investment attracting tax relief.

Vocational training payments. Relief given for approved vocational courses.

Widow's bereavement allowance. An allowance given to widows (not widowers) for two tax years after their husband dies.

Index